The Death of the Author and Anticolonial Thought

Michael R. Griffiths

The Death of the Author and Anticolonial Thought

palgrave
macmillan

Michael R. Griffiths
School of The Arts, English and Media
University of Wollongong
Wollongong, NSW, Australia

ISBN 978-3-031-80907-1   ISBN 978-3-031-80908-8 (eBook)
https://doi.org/10.1007/978-3-031-80908-8

© The Editor(s) (if applicable) and The Author(s), under exclusive license to Springer Nature Switzerland AG 2025

This work is subject to copyright. All rights are solely and exclusively licensed by the Publisher, whether the whole or part of the material is concerned, specifically the rights of translation, reprinting, reuse of illustrations, recitation, broadcasting, reproduction on microfilms or in any other physical way, and transmission or information storage and retrieval, electronic adaptation, computer software, or by similar or dissimilar methodology now known or hereafter developed.

The use of general descriptive names, registered names, trademarks, service marks, etc. in this publication does not imply, even in the absence of a specific statement, that such names are exempt from the relevant protective laws and regulations and therefore free for general use.

The publisher, the authors and the editors are safe to assume that the advice and information in this book are believed to be true and accurate at the date of publication. Neither the publisher nor the authors or the editors give a warranty, expressed or implied, with respect to the material contained herein or for any errors or omissions that may have been made. The publisher remains neutral with regard to jurisdictional claims in published maps and institutional affiliations.

Cover illustration: © Melisa Hasan

This Palgrave Macmillan imprint is published by the registered company Springer Nature Switzerland AG
The registered company address is: Gewerbestrasse 11, 6330 Cham, Switzerland

If disposing of this product, please recycle the paper.

Epigraph

I'm gonna break up this signifyin', somebody's gotta go.
—Sonny Boy Williamson

In this typology, the category of intention will not disappear; it will have its place, but from this place it will no longer be able to govern the entire scene and the entire system of utterances.[1]
—Jacques Derrida

Derrida himself is a brilliant philosopher and critic, and he can't be responsible for what people made of his notions. But to use the deconstructive techniques as a substitute for genetic analysis is, I think, a serious error in perception and judgement. Nothing in a text merely occurs or happens; a text is made—by the author, the critic, the reader—and it is a collective enterprise to a certain extent.[2]
—Edward Said

---

[1] Jacques Derrida, "Signature, Event, Context," in *Margins of Philosophy*. Trans. Alan Bass. Chicago: U. of Chicago, P, 1972, 326.

[2] Edward Said, "Beginnings," in *Power, Politics and Culture: Interviews with Edward Said*. London: Bloomsbury, 2004, 18.

The poetic intention has always brought us to the absolute prescience of the Whole-world.[3]

—Édouard Glissant

[3] Édouard Glissant, "In Praise of the Different and of Difference," trans. Celia Britton, Callaloo 34, no. 4 (2013): 856-62, 860.

Acknowledgments

It was Betty Joseph at Rice University who suggested I look at Édouard Glissant in around 2011 or so and Stathis Gourgouris at Columbia University a few years later who suggested I take a look at Edward Said's *Beginnings*. I thank each of them.

The following colleagues read this work, providing invaluable feedback: Guy Davidson, Cath McKinnon, Ned Curthoys, Paul Sharrad, Lauren Weber, Joseph Steinberg, James Faubion, Emma Darragh and Louis Klée (who helped give the book its eventual name). I thank also the two readers for Palgrave (who were anonymous at that time), who most generously but also critically offered feedback on an earlier version of the manuscript: Anna Bernard and David Ventura.

Other colleagues have engaged with this work in other ways, including at academic conferences and presentations or through informal and enriching conversations, these include: Alex Trimble Young, Graham Akhurst, Blayne Welsh, Jonathan Dunk, Evelyn Araluen, Mat Wall-Smith, Tim Bruniges, Aaron Burton, Dashiell Moore, Charlotte Okkes-Sane, Micaela Sahhar. Blayne and Graham: the yarns we had about storytelling really helped me and inform particularly the conclusion of the book. Thank you!

Parts of the book were written in the Autumn of 2023 while I was on a visiting fellowship at the Centre for Advancement in Indigenous Knowledges at the University of Technology, Sydney. Thanks are greatly due to Heidi Norman as director and Graham Akhurst for facilitating this opportunity. Other academic staff with whom I interacted showed collegiality and warmth and there was no doubt some cross-pollination that affected my work for the best. I thank Lea Lui-Chivizhe, Anne Maree Payne, Katrina Thorpe, and Archie Thomas for this.

A version of the chapter on Said was presented through AUHE in 2023; thanks are due to Chris Danta for organising that series. Another version of the same talk was workshopped at UOW through the Centre for Creative Critical Practice (C3P) in the same year.

There is a story of intentions being shaped on my part in the long range of years that formed this project. Growing up I had always had a vague sense that the situation of Palestine (like that in Australia where I was born) was a settler colonial one, even if I had little sense of the history of occupation and dispossession in detail. Just so, I came to know Edward Said's work as a critic of Empire and of course on Orientalism during my undergraduate years, but I did not know in my youth of his concrete situation as an exile in Cairo and then the United States from the land of Palestine which was his family's home. Hence it was only in my Ph.D. study at Rice University that I really began to educate myself on the details of these matters. This was due in no small part to the influence of a person I consider a friend to this day, the anthropologist Ala Alazzeh, my classmate at Rice and now a professor at Birzeit University. We had known each other a few years when he came to live at the share house I resided at while he prepared to return to the West Bank for his ethnographic fieldwork. This was late in December of 2008, which some will recall was the midst of what the IDF called "Operation Cast Lead," a military assault on the Gaza Strip that, amongst other things would later come to be recognised as a case of war crimes for the use of white phosphorous on civilians. Ala stayed up through the night in the days of January 2009, glued to a brutal news cycle and as often in contact with friends and family as he could be. It was around the time of this intensification of occupation that I came to understand something Ala had conveyed to me earlier in 2008. Ala and I had come together with the intention of forming a reading group at Rice on settler colonialism. In drafting the group's statement, we realised we had a difference of analytic viewpoint. I, a student of theory from a privileged settler background, wanted to emphasise a Foucauldian viewpoint, situated around structures of power. Ala, a refugee, born in a camp in Bethlehem insisted: "this violence," he said, "this occupation is intentional." I continue to learn the importance of this insight.

Contents

1	**The Deaths of the Author**	1
	Before the Death of the Author	5
	The Death of the Author	7
	After the Death of the Author	12
	The Death of the Author and Anticolonial Thought	18
2	**"With the Intention of Opening Up the Future": Decolonial Authorship Before Barthes' Essay**	27
3	**The Ghost of the Writer: Édouard Glissant's Poetics of the Whole-World**	39
	Poetic Intention after the "Death of the Author"	44
	Opacity, the Unsayable, and the Vow of the Other	50
4	**An Appetite to Begin: Intention and the Political in the Work of Edward Said**	67
	Two Visions in (and Around) Beginnings	72
	The Politics of World and Text	79
	Empire and Intention	84
5	**On Writing, Storytelling, Community**	93
	Index	105

CHAPTER 1

The Deaths of the Author

Abstract This opening chapter explores the background to the notion of the death of the author and the debates around this postulate. Turning back to much earlier developments that lay the ground work for Barthes' pronouncement such as key ideas from Matthew Arnold and, in the twentieth century the ideas of Wimsatt and Beardsley such as the "intentional fallacy." The chapter then gives a detailed reading of Barthes' essay and of Foucault's "What is an Author," in order to situate the reader in relation to the analysis to follow. It then surveys works of criticism that have thematized these developments subsequently including work by Seàn Burke, Judith Ryan, Mark McGurl, Timothy Bewes, and others. The final section surveys key concepts such as decolonization itself as well as related analysis of literary intention from a black and decolonizing perspective in the early work of Henry Louis Gates Jr. This survey of the debates thus sets up the chapters to follow in their discussion of challenges to the death of the author postulate.

Keywords Authorship · Death of the author · Intentional fallacy · Signification · Decolonization

An author nearly died in 2022. Salman Rushdie, the author of (with most relevance) *The Satanic Verses* had, for some thirty-five years, found

© The Author(s), under exclusive license to Springer Nature Switzerland AG 2025
M. R. Griffiths, *The Death of the Author and Anticolonial Thought*,
https://doi.org/10.1007/978-3-031-80908-8_1

the threat of a religious edict sentencing him to death hanging over his head, when in August of that year he was stabbed on stage at a speaking event; an attack he survived. Rushdie had spent seven years in hiding after the 1988 fatwā that was issued calling for his death, before he finally began emerging for public appearances in 1995. After the death of the Iranian Ayatollah Khomenei in the late 1990s the fatwā was weakened, though not lifted; it was reinstated in 2005. There is so much to say about Rushdie and the fatwā—more than I wish to discuss could be identified as relevant here. Rushdie's novel could be seen to have offended Muslims on a number of counts, from the way a scribe in its narrative—named, in an intriguing moment almost of *mise en abyme*, Salman the Persian—finds himself questioning the proclamations of a prophet called Mahound (a variant of Mohammed) in an ancient desert city called Jahilia. Along with this we find a fictional harem naming its female employees after Mahound's wives and much else that satirically echoes and troubles the early days of Islam. It is not my intention here to provide a complete chronicle of the way Rushdie naively or actively, defensibly or offensively set out to refract the world of religion and, in particular, Islam, in his 1988 novel. Nor is it my intention to chronicle the world outside the text, the world of controversy and contention, violence and approbation that carries us from Pakistan to India to Iran after the revolution to the response to the fatwā in Thatcher's Britain on up.

This is not, therefore, a book about Rushdie's near death, his survival, or even his novels. It is a book about a highly connected concept: the death of the author—Roland Barthes' concept (and related structuralist and poststructuralist claims) and their reception in writing by anticolonial thinkers—a topic that Rushdie's brush with death effectively literalizes and illustrates. This book is, then, an analysis in several case studies of the way such anticolonial thinkers have engaged with, critiqued, and even adopted the lessons and limitations of the poststructuralist analysis of that most fetishized and also reviled of figures: the author.

The Death of the Author and Anticolonial Thought aims to account for the response of anticolonial thinkers—by which I meant those whose thought and sometimes action opposed colonization and its legacies—to the influence of the death of the author postulate and related poststructuralist declarations. From almost the moment Roland Barthes made his famous declaration of the death of the author, the notion was contested and frequently in the realm of anticolonial thought. Such near contemporary responses to poststructuralist claims about the author's "death," which is to say redundancy from the act of interpretation, include the principle subjects of this book: Martinican poet and thinker Édouard Glissant and Palestinian literary and cultural critic Edward Said. This book, then, examines the immediate emergence and intensification of such responses to the postulate of the author's deathly absence from the text, in order to suggest that metropolitan literary theory drew the critique and contribution of scholars from black, decolonial, and global south perspectives almost from the get go. Indeed, my first chapter shows examples of anticolonial writers championing the figure of the author even in the years preceding Barthes's declaration, drawing on earlier critiques of authorship in order to oppose them and in doing so, anticipating and objecting to Barthes's influential framing of the question. Figures engaged in this early exploration include Wilson Harris and, notably, Frantz Fanon.

But, this is not to cast Rushdie aside. To tarry a moment longer with this author as an acute example of what is perhaps the situation for authorship as such: How can even the near-dead author be hermeneutically done away with? How could one begin to think through this author's texts (in particular) without a sense of what has happened to him, the context in which he speaks, the offense he has caused, his south Asian Muslim background, the Islam he now renounces, etc. The influence of Rushdie as an author and his tenacious survival against a violent attack cannot be understood only in terms of biography, or, conversely, in terms of his texts. Perhaps the best we could hope to do is partially illuminate them contrapuntally, as perhaps only Anshuman Mondal has done.[1] What Said called contrapuntal reading draws on music theory to suggest a form of rhythmic play with contrast—like a timpani, developing two themes at different tempos and dynamic levels. More generally, the idea that the author is dead and, more accurately, that the contexts and paratexts that s/he has generated are irrelevant—since nothing but the text is—suggests a totally narrow avenue of interpretation. Rushdie criticism—particularly that which seriously attempts a reading of *The Satanic Verses*—would seem sorely lacking if it attempted to read this text in isolation from the text's affiliations, to use a powerful term of Said's. For Said, what we inherit from vertical relations such as those stemming from a nation or from one's family (all of which he calls filiation) are often less powerful than the horizontal relations one experiences across broader sets of connections such as through class, culture, and aesthetic taste—the latter triad of exempla which he names affiliation.[2] Rushdie's filiation from Islam, but also his affiliation to Britain and to India, to the modernities of either, and to a secularism of its moment have each of course been crucial to his epitextual persona. Rushdie's novel(s) cannot be read without a sense of context, history, and even Koranic and other religious hermeneutics but also, a certain attention to the spectral presence of the author.[3]

This author and many authors like him are not dead, yet they and the paratexts they produced are nonetheless at times passed over in the search for their texts' meaning. It is an assumption of the present book—*The Death of the Author and Anticolonial Thought*— that context, paratext, and all those marks and signs that point to and implicate a figure we call the author are absolutely essential in literary criticism. More urgently, perhaps, it is the case that authors from decolonizing backgrounds have been putting caveats to the death of the author hypothesis, essentially since its inception. In this way, this book is a partial, cultural history and, in being so, it is more an account of how others have done this than a theoretical elaboration of some transcendentally effective methodology for treating authorship. The book tells a story about the way key thinkers—foregrounding two Martinican thinkers and one Palestinian, each at the center of an example set that refers to several others—engaged with, critiqued, built upon, and contested metropolitan (particularly, French) literary theories about authorship and such related ideas as questions of discourse, structure, and agency in the relation between text and world. Said and Glissant were each authors from marginal backgrounds who found large audiences in the metropolitan center. For each of them in different ways, the emphasis on the pure textual play promised by the death of the author, while exciting, elided critical dimensions of what authorship, presence, and intention had previously offered. From Glissant's perspective (as we shall see at greater length in Chapter 2), the black Caribbean writer would, with the loss of authorship, find himself unmoored—the presence he had just earned from the colonies effaced at the exact moment he earned it. Yet, for Glissant, authorship had never been the individualistic enterprise that Barthes sought so provocatively to efface: for the former, the figure of the writer emerged really only in relation to the work and, importantly, to a community in relation to which they were engaged. This emphasis on community and on, in particular, revisable manifestations of beginning in relation to it was differently evident, also in Said's engagement with the question of the author. For Said, literary "intention" is not simply an isolated proposition, but rather, "the link between idiosyncratic view and the communal concern."[4] Intention is, then, the link between our individual traits and quirks and the audience (or the author's conception of the audience) who would consume them. Said's theory of beginnings is not only a theory of intention but one that describes the social meaning of the way authors internalize their audiences, their very cultures.

What emerges from this story about authorship, told from the perspective of anticolonial intellectuals is the degree to which a richer, more profound story about literary authorship is possible when the object of analysis (and indeed, approbation) is not the individual author of capitalist modernity witnessed by Barthes. In the years immediately following Barthes' essay, Glissant and Said show how authorship has always been complex and multiple, relating to many forms of self and most of all to the community of intellectuals from whom the authorial self emerges and whom they themselves address. Indeed, as I have begun to describe, I show in Chapter 1 how anticolonial authors like Fanon and Harris had been making this case even prior to Barthes' essay's publication. In the 1950s and early 1960s writings by Harris and Fanon anticipate the vehemence of Barthes' critique as they each emphasized a humanist embrace of authorial imprint and communal representation.

The notion of the death of the author, promulgated in this particular locution by Barthes in 1967 has endured because it is at once enticing and overdetermined. It is enticing because it emphasizes the primacy of an immensely productive activity: close reading, a focus on the text itself and its significations; it is overdetermined by a series of prohibitions that bely the freedom suggested in such textual play. One of the first things to note is that the birth of the death of the author (so to speak) as an idea, which, while it began life as a revolutionary refusal of critical writing vested in such forms of scholarship as emphasized the "life and works" of an author, has now hardened into dogma with a rejection of authorial presence *tout court*.

BEFORE THE DEATH OF THE AUTHOR

Zadie Smith, in an essay on Barthes and Nabokov points out that, "it's easy to read 'The Death of the Author' as a series of revolutionary demands, but it's worth remembering that it was also simply a licked forefinger held up to test a wind already blowing."[5] In this way, the genealogy of the notion of the death of the author is one both long in duration and recent in the influence it maintains (upon its exponents as well as its detractors). For instance, the idea of the irrelevance of the author's own ideas, background, and prejudices is something of a piece with Matthew Arnold's idea about the *disinteredness* of the critic, promulgated most famously and sustainedly in the 1864 essay "The Function of Criticism at the Present Time."[6] Arnold believed that the exercise of the creative faculties was the pinnacle that human endeavor could attain. In that 1864 essay, Arnold asserts that criticism itself can approach the lofty heights of the human mind he associates with the creative act if it avoids the excesses of political partisanship and the practical in favor of its own natural inclinations. As he asked, rhetorically:

> How is criticism to show disinterestedness? By keeping aloof from what is called 'the practical view of things;' by resolutely following the law of its own nature, which is to be a free play of the mind on all subjects on which it touches. By steadily refusing to lend itself to any of those ulterior, political, practical considerations about ideas, which plenty of people will be sure to attach to them.[7]

Arnold's notion of disinterestedness distinguishes the critic by an appeal to the "free play of the mind"—an elusive notion emphasizing a critical reason that belies the personal "ulterior political, practical considerations" that imply partiality and situatedness. This is not, of course, the same as the sacrifice of the personal partiality of the author but it is, I suggest, vested in a related sense of impartiality: one beginning with the critic's faculties and not the text's play or the intentions of the author—nor indeed her unconscious. The very notion of "free play" is, however, shared between Arnold's argument about criticism and what one finds in various guises in both the New Criticism of the middle twentieth century in the United States and in what has come to be known as French poststructuralism as each emphasizes the free play of the text, its primacy, the movement of trace and iterability, the author function, and on and on.[8]

So what of the New Critics, then? Of their relation to prototypical literary theory? Several key figures who entered this theoretical mold (rather than basing their conjectures only on the paradigm of the movement: close reading) were William K. Wimsatt and Monroe C. Beardsley. In their 1946 essay "The Intentional Fallacy" and their 1949 sequel, "The Affective Fallacy," the pair suggested crucial limitations to the scope of interpretation; limitations designed to focus close reading on its essential goal of textual meaning. As the historian of literary ideas, Chris Baldick puts it, "[f]or Wimsatt and Beardsley in 'The Intentional Fallacy,' the poem (or other text) 'belongs' not only to the author but to the public, and by entering the realm of language has released itself from the author's power to control meanings. The author's prior intention is either unavailable to us—except as transformed into the work itself—or, if separately available, superseded by the work."[9] Echoing what Barthes would later call the "birth of the reader" (though not, in the same way, entirely approvingly) Wimsatt and Beardsley's notion of "The Affective Fallacy" provides a counterpoint to the intentional fallacy in that it debunk the "fallacious confusion between the poem and its psychological effects ('affects') upon reason."[10] In this way, whereas the intentional fallacy marks the risk of seeking the outcome of close reading (and other kinds of reading) in the author's intentions, the affective fallacy arises when the reader's subjective impressions are taken as the paramount basis for the accrual and generation of meaning in literary analysis. Just as there was critical work prior to Barthes that anticipated his notion of the death of the author, so there existed criticism by anticolonial writers that grappled with problem that Harris attributes to Lukacs: the problem that, "creative work may, and often does have entirely different meanings to what the author hopes."[11] This is the subject of my first chapter. Nonetheless, the licked forefinger Smith calls attention to can everywhere detect the breeze of skepticism about the figure of the author, but Barthes' essay would unleash a true whirlwind in the face of which authorial intention and presence would not easily resist.

The Death of the Author

It isn't hard (these days, at least) to accept the most crucial objections Barthes makes in his 1967 lecture to what he calls our "attach[ment] to the person of the author."[12] It isn't hard to accept—indeed, it seems quite natural—and this is not the least because from English Literature departments (and even in many cases) to Creative Writing programs, the idea of the death of the author has become something of an orthodoxy. Smith notes that, when she teaches Barthes' text, it divides her students in two; but it still continues to be taught as a foundational text for students of writing and of reading.[13] As Barthes notes, so often before (and even since) his intervention, students and scholars seek to locate: "[t]he explanation of a work [...] in the man or woman who produced it, as if it were always in the end, through the more or less transparent allegory of the fiction, the voice of a single person, the *author* 'confiding' in us."[14] Barthes uses as examples certain forms of narration given in particular to intransitive locutions—such as a moment of ambiguity he draws from the nineteenth-century French realist writer Honoré de Balzac—and, we can add, (various modes of) free indirect discourse. He suggests that in these forms, the ambiguity surrounding the question, "who speaks" makes the presence of the author increasingly uncertain, even irrelevant. In a key passage, he frames the matter as follows:

> No doubt it has always been that way. As soon as a fact is *narrated* no longer with a view to acting directly on reality but intransitively, that is to say, finally outside of any function other than that of the very practice of the symbol itself, this disconnection occurs, the voice loses its origin, the author enters into his own death, writing begins.[15]

Who could dispute the precision present in this provocation? Indeed anyone who has taught literature has detected in students, even perhaps among colleagues, the curious "attachment to the author" Barthes identifies. We tend, it seems, to employ the idea of the death of the author tactically for the most part—an intervention designed to focus student attention on the text rather than leaving this to lapse into a vulgar sense that the text represents a mere projection of the author's psyche. Yet has it always been this way? With some critical irony, Barthes revises his statement:

> The sense of this phenomenon, however, has varied; in ethnographic societies the responsibility for a narrative is never assumed by a person but by a mediator, shaman or relator whose 'performance' - the mastery of the narrative code may possibly be admired but never his 'genius'. The author is a modem figure a product of our society insofar as, emerging from the Middle Ages with English empiricism, French rationalism and the personal faith of the Reformation, it discovered the prestige of the individual, of, as it is more nobly put, the 'human person'. It is thus logical that in literature it. should be this positivism, the epitome and culmination of capitalist ideology, which has attached the greatest importance to the 'person' of the author.[16]

In this way, Barthes crucially historicizes the emergence of the author function, differentiating creative practice more generally from its form as "the 'person' of the author" in "capitalist ideology" in its contemporary, fetishized instantiation. When taking into account, Barthes suggests, that the author is merely a function of the text—the one that says "I" in an intransitive relation to the real—one can see (even now, with its relative status as dogma) the powerful implications of this assertion. As Barthes himself says,

> The removal of the Author (one could talk here with Brecht of a veritable 'distancing,' the Author diminishing like a figurine at the far end of the literary stage) is not merely an historical fact or an act of writing; it utterly transforms the modem text (or - which is the same thing the text is henceforth made and read in such a way that at all its levels the author is absent).[17]

The death of the author, for Barthes, releases the limit that an external author imposes on the text and allows for an extensive play with meaning on the part of the interpreter.[18] As the famous phrase has it, the "death of the author" is the condition for the "birth of the reader"—or, to give the text its full context:

> We are now beginning to let ourselves be fooled no longer by the arrogant antiphrastical recriminations of good society in favour of the very thing it sets aside, ignores, smothers, or destroys; we know that to give writing its future, it is necessary to overthrow the myth: the birth of the reader must be at the cost of the death of the Author.[19]

In declaring the death of the author and combining this postulate with that of the birth of the reader, Barthes precipitated a revolution, probably even more so than Wimsatt and Beardsley and I mean this last claim to include that the former was more influential than the latter two have been even within the Anglo-American literary studies academy. But what is the temporal dimension that animates this call to revolution? Barthes's description of "ethnographic" backgrounds and those of the "Middle Ages," transformed toward the condition of capitalist personhood and individual authorship by English empiricism, French rationalism, and the Reformation, each also punctuating that caveat to his (almost) symptomatic reading of Balzac: "No doubt it has always been that way." Could it be that the logic of the text has always been paramount and, indeed, extricable from the function of the "I?" This would be quite a feat within the "ethnographic societies" that Barthes describes—with some perceptiveness—as emphasizing the custodianship (the shaman as a "mediator") and performance of stories held by the community. It is apt that we note that this question cannot be answered by a mere reading of Barthes' text. Needless to say, Barthes is both holding up "ethnographic societies" as a transformative example and (possibly) rendering them analogous to the modern play with text that will be emphasized by him in a poet such as Mallarmé.

One question to ask is: What happens when the colonized person is also an author? As First Nations (Goorie) novelist from Australia, Melissa Lucashenko has asserted: "The author is not dead and the Aboriginal author is certainly not dead. A double happiness."[20] Similarly, in an essay in the radical Australian literary journal *Overland*, Wiradjuri author Jeanine Leane takes aim dialectically at two consequences of Barthes' essay: its whiteness on the one hand and the way its openness to the reader can serve as a justification to appropriation. As Leane writes:

> [For Barthes] the essential meaning of a work depends on the impressions of the reader, rather than the passions or tastes of the writer; a text's unity lies not in its origins, or its creator, but in its destination, or its audience. This view aptly sums the long trajectory of European appropriation, blindness to its own cultural standpoint, western literary colonialism, and the consumption of minority cultures by invading, colonising powers.[21]

For Leane, then, the birth of the reader always carries the potential for appropriation. What happens, we may further ask, when sacred tradition and story are (partially) rendered in a form such as the novel or particular kinds of experimental poem by Indigenous writers themselves? Are these authors dead along with the kin and Country they manifest in text. In other words, Barthes both employs the figure of the "ethnographic society" as a convenient point of contrast and opens up the beginning of these questions (even as he does not himself explore them).

At a lecture at the College de France in 1969 that represents both an autonomous elaboration and, in part, a response to Barthes, Michel Foucault emphasizes the relation between the "function" of the author as a discursive operation and the various ways an *oeuvre* (both as an individual work or body of work) is made up.[22] As he insists there, the "disappearance—or death—of the author" does not simply free the critic from the taxonomy of the work and its limits—it does though give birth to the reader as a free, playful subject engaging with a limitlessly open text.[23] For Foucault, "[i]t is not enough to declare that we should do without the writer (the author) and study the work itself. The word work and the unity that it designates are probably as problematic as the status of the author's individuality."[24] In this moment of clear departure from Barthes and his essay, Foucault moves the terms of the debate from author to work and in doing so, anchors the discussion in the relation between the "proper name" of the author as the name of a biographical subject and, more pertinently the proper name of the author and the "author's name" as an index of the author's work. To be sure, Foucault's text is in accord with Barthes on the restrictiveness of a certain idea of the author in terms of textual meaning. The former says in concluding: "[t]he author is the principle of thrift in the proliferation of meaning."[25] This is so, even as there is already a certain defiance of Barthes' provocation on Foucault's part, a sense of the former's simplification, an urgency to taxonomize and enumerate the various conditions by which the function of the author defines the contours and stakes of writing in the fields of not only the humanities but what in France were called the "human sciences" (*sciences humaines*).

But, for me, what is perhaps even more intriguing is Foucault's mode of exemplification. Like Barthes, with his figure of the Shaman, coming as it does alongside such modernist experimenters as Mallarmé, Foucault draws on examples of unusual formations of the work that are not themselves, European. After a brief mention of the Greek Epic, Foucault's next key example and a key problem text for the question of authorship is *The Thousand and One Nights*. He describes the text as a problem of both authorship—(since the original) "author" from the Islamic Golden Age is unknown—and for the question of whether such a body of stories "constitutes a work." Further clearly this body of work—if it is one—is held together by a fictional storyteller Scheherezade: the teller of the tales that follow. That Scheherezade is telling these tales to preserve her very life is not immaterial to Foucault. Indeed, he draws from this to emphasize the relation between writing and death more generally. As he puts it:

> In another way, the motivation, as well as the theme and the pretext of Arabian narratives—such as *The Thousand and One Nights*—was also the eluding of death: one spoke, telling stories into the early morning, in order to forestall death, to postpone the day of reckoning that would silence the

narrator. Scheherazade's narrative is an effort, renewed each night, to keep death outside the circle of life.[26]

The Thousand and One Nights, with its frame narrative portraying survival as storytelling, is often read as lacking contextual detail, authorship, etc., (despite shelves of scholarship that has addressed these questions). The experience of reading the Arabian Nights (as it is colloquially known) maintains the spectral authority of Scheherezade herself even as she is the frame narrator and not the author. In this way, the diegetic tension between the possible and absent authors, Scheherezade, and all such aspects of the text that depend on sincerity and authority is so often transmitted and received as mysterious. *The Thousand and One Nights*, then, is a paradigmatic text in considering the author function but its circumstances of authorship also make it an exception as is the case with other texts where knowledge of the author—even the author's name—is absent. This is so, for instance, in the original *Nibulungenleid* of around 1200CE, for example; it is arguably the case given how relatively little epitextual material is available on and about Jane Austen. But I am exercised by the example of Scheherezade that is given by Foucault and particularly so since it comes from outside Europe. Indeed, Foucault's example set is wide ranging but *The Thousand and One Nights* remains the most prominent of the few non-European examples. Foucault's use of *The Thousand and One Nights* makes of the exceptional paradox of authorship and oriental mystery: one occupied with the relation between death and storytelling more widely. For both Barthes and Foucault, the question of the author is a modern one and its limit cases are set in contrast to the ancient, the non-European, the other.

AFTER THE DEATH OF THE AUTHOR

Zadie Smith's perception that Barthes' essay represents principally the "licked forefinger" of a sensibility about authorship that was already in the process of emerging is one thing. But the reaction against Barthes' essay blows cold air on that forefinger from another direction. The notion of the death of the author has, in this way, had its detractors in Anglophone literary criticism, as early as Seàn Burke, who patiently works through Barthes' writing on the topic (along with that of Foucault and Jacques Derrida on related notions of authorship and intention, signature, event, and context). Burke points convincingly to the way that though Barthes manifested the death of the author and centered it in his 1967 essay alongside its important converse—the birth of the reader—his own subsequent work relied heavily on a version of scholarship interested in the persona of the author.[27] For instance, according to Burke, in Barthes' book *Sade, Fourier, Loyola* the authors under Barthes' gaze—the Marquis de Sade, the utopian social theorist Charles Fourier, and the Jesuit Saint Ignatius of Loyola—are not only essential to his reading of their work but he views each of them as a "founder of language."[28] As Burke puts it, limning Barthes with some irony, for the latter: "[i]f a text has been 'unglued' of its referentiality, its author need not die; to the contrary, he can flourish, become an object of autobiographical pleasure, perhaps even a 'founder of language.'"[29] For Barthes, the death of the author was less the progenitor of the reader, in all her or his free play. Rather, perhaps, what the death of the author gave rise to in some select cases was rather the lofty figures known as the founder of language. As Jane Gallop has noted, however, the relation of the author to their literal and metaphorical deaths is a temporal relation and one which often gives rise to an even more fecund discussion of the authorial subject.[30]

In the last fifteen or so years, several studies have appeared that consider late twentieth-century writing in relation to the impact of the idea of the death of the author. The earliest of these, Judith Ryan, suggested in her *The Novel After Theory* that while varying critiques and caveats to authorial intention had existed since Wimsatt and Beardsley and arguably before, Barthes' essay has taken the idea the furthest, not even granting "the author as a point of origin for the text."[31] Further and more urgently, Ryan makes the case for the impact of Barthes', Derrida's, and Foucault's ideas about authorship on contemporary writing in the half century or so following their emergence in the late 1960s, tracking this influence and impact through such writers of the mid-twentieth century as Alain Robbe-Grillet, Margaret Duras, and more recent authors such as W. G. Sebald and J. M. Coetzee. More recent critics such as Aryan Arya and Philip Sayer follow similar critical itineraries to Ryan, taking seriously, as Sayers puts it, writing in the "wake" of Barthes and "the death of the author."[32] Each critic has a differing set of reference points through this accounting of influence with Sayer, for instance playfully comparing Smith and Judith Butler while Arya's post-1945 trajectory puts him into a position of seeing Barthes' assertion as a strong part of a wave anticipated in figures such as Beckett. Nonetheless, while Arya turns in his last chapter to globalization and Ryan makes an intriguing case for the groundedness of Derrida's key essay "Structure, Sign. And Play," in his origins as a French Jew growing up in Algeria (further analogizing this experience to that of Duras as a French citizen born in Indochina), the question of colonialism and anticolonial thought is little considered in this literature.[33] *The Death of the Author and Anticolonial Thought* makes the case for a counter-current of ways of thinking about the author, the subject, and the human in the years straddling Barthes' declaration.

Other recent debates have attended upon authorship also. For instance, one recent detractor of the death of the author premise, Mark McGurl, has been entirely dismissive of the postulate, as it disconnects authorship from the "programs," of the current era: the creative writing schools and the systems of instruction that inform them:

> The indeterminacy of the relation between author and character is in this case quite real, a matter of pragmatic fact, but to make it a principle (whether by way of prohibitions against the 'biographical fallacy,' as the New Critics called it, or in the absurd declarations of the 'death of the author' that were heard in the 1960s) is to risk missing one of the most basic dynamics of postwar literary production.[34]

McGurl's dismissal of the death of the author, the biographical fallacy, the intentional fallacy, and so on, is well founded in a particular line of reasoning, namely that the creative economy, with its commodification of experience benefits from the assertion of "personal indetermination" in art.

Meanwhile, detractors of the death of the author hypothesis such as McGurl have their own critics in turn. Timothy Bewes, in an effort to "to ground a conception of the novel as a mode of thought," has extensively critiqued the relevance of authorship to any conception of the novel that would take on board the sort of connectedness and disjuncture, indeterminacy, and anti-exemplarity that he finds displayed in contemporary "postfiction" from Rachel Cusk to an author we have encountered, Zadie Smith.[35] As Bewes puts it, limning Lukacs's notion of the historico-philosophical:

> In a historico-philosophical approach, entities such as the writer's beliefs or intentions, or the question of his or her complicity in dominant ideologies, or the sense of an underlying political agenda, while no doubt operative in

the work's composition, are not derivable from a reading of the work. Nor, therefore, can they be held to have any explanatory privilege regarding its meaning.

Allow me to take momentary issue with the (perhaps defensible) conjecture that the politics of a text's (or its author's) context are "not derivable from a reading of the work." This may be so but its logical tie to the idea that context yields no "explanatory privilege" does not follow analytically from it. The answer lies of course not in a critique of this logic but with a third path: The politics of a text's generative context might not have a *privileged* role in deciding on textual meaning, *but among many techniques its role is essential*. While any interpretation goes in an undergraduate classroom (the very paradigm of the birth of the reader), in many such contexts interpretations whither on the vine of contextual pressure, most obviously such issues as historical anachronism, but also under pressure from a good knowledge of the politics of a text's epitexts. Bewes continues, however:

> Likewise, aesthetic values like authenticity or sincerity, and even legal concepts such as plagiarism, do not register at the historico-philosophical level other than as formal phenomena, "resolutions" that depend for their unity on the unverifiable claims of an individual consciousness. Historico-philosophically, then, the subjective (conceptual, thematic) dimensions of a work do not coincide with the work's substance, even when such elements expand within the novel form, giving the work an "essayistic" quality and seeming to carry a large burden of readerly interest.[36]

What is named here in Lukascian terms as "historico-philosophical" aims to compass not only the text in splendid isolation (the "philosophical" level on which the text thinks) but also the historical level of context. It is not only that Bewes divides historical context (claiming it has no purchase) from the text, but it is also the case that his division rests on individual consciousness being separated from the text. However, it is almost as if "individual consciousness's" relation to text is a priori impossible for Bewes. What could have been a limitation or a caveat becomes an eviscerating factor in the potential link between individual consciousness and text. Without presaging too much about what I say throughout this book, I follow Said, Glissant, and others in beginning with "individual consciousness" or intention while recognizing that it is at times disinscribed, written out, or lost to textual play, rather than inadmissible in advance.

At any rate, Bewes takes particular issue with McGurl, a putative McGurl predecessor in mid-twentieth century critic Wayne C. Booth, and progenitor of the distant reading approach Franco Moretti.[37] The struggles of these critics against any role for authorship as such smack of the same kind of rejections that have always been leveled at defenders of any method that maintains some modicum of relation between text and author (or, for that matter, text and critic). Bewes writes "In Booth and McGurl this subjectivism is manifested in the intentionality of the author, whereas for Moretti, sovereignty is located with the reader."[38] Bewes continues, claiming that:

> there is an extraordinary, unbridgeable gap in contemporary criticism around the question of expression, in which even those critics who insist that the final point of reference for the critic is the author and his or her intentions are unable, on that basis, to say much else about the work other than to allude to its 'excellence' and in which those who locate everything of critical significance away from the author and the text do so on the basis of 'a sort of cosmic and inevitable division of labour.'[39]

There is a great deal to either side of the McGurl-Bewes debate—indeed, there may be some relevance of each position in the context of a very North Atlantic understanding of creative writing in the era of late capitalism and indeed, beyond. Bewes and McGurl each have valuable things to say, to be sure. While McGurl sees the author as a product of a sociocultural milieu (and for him this is the writing program that dominates today), Bewes wants to return to the autonomous novel and its mode of expression in spite of authorship. However, the North Atlantic is not the world in its totality and writers who take their orientation from and locate their origin in the decolonial perspectives of the Global South have, I will suggest, long unpicked the notion that the author is dead, the Foucauldian author function or indeed the Derridean "signature." Neither Bewes nor McGurl have a theory of the author, they each have a theory that either dismisses or avoids this figure. The gambit of this book is that the key representative figures from the global south I have selected: Edward Said, Édouard Glissan, do have theories of what an author is and what intention is (and it is a good thing that they do). A further gambit lies in the fact that refusals of the now orthodox diminution of authorship in the act of interpretation *are not new* for anticolonial thinkers. It therefore aims to explore all of the numerous anticolonial refusals of the death of the author idea (and they are many) but frames the immediate lead-up to Barthes' essay in Harris and Fanon before it hones the immediate—if indirect—response Said and Glissant, in the years immediately following Barthes' intervention. Furthermore, as we will see, both Said and Glissant had crucial caveats to offer to the idea of the death of the author in the years following Barthes' essay. And, to be clear, while each names the category of intention, neither figure means it to instruct their reader in anything as reductive as a merely evaluative category such as "excellence." Nor does intention, for any of these anticolonial thinkers (though with particular complexity in Said and Glissant), reduce to a simplistic account of the biographical subject or to a phenomenologically vague view of intention. What their arguments do develop out of such ideas as beginning intention (Said) and an intention that "perfects itself in relation" (Glissant) are ideas that, suffice it to say, are reducible to neither the capitalist author subject that trouble Barthes or those worries Bewes has with McGurl's argument. One key contention of this book and also its principle topos is that almost as soon as the idea of the death of the author was alive in the world, for instance as Barthes' (doubtless) revolutionary essay appeared in 1967, at least a few anticolonial authors were taking on board its lessons and rejecting its limitations; numerous authors from the global south have continued to develop critiques of this notion ever since.

This book, then avows that the idea of the death of the author, aligned as it is to modern and postmodern sensibilities emerges as a particular response to capitalism, intellectual property, and the publishing industry—McGurl would say so, Barthes more or less already did! It is my further contention that the emancipatory potential of the death of the author postulate is shadowed always by its denial of experience. That the historical moment of the death of the author's 1967 pronouncement is coincident with the emergence of the successful decolonial movements of the global South is no accident either. In the years leading up to Barthes' pronouncement, Ghana and India, Kenya and Algeria—to name a few—sued for decolonized relations to the colonial and imperial powers in whose sphere they had long been held: from attempts at full independence to departmentalization to thwarted resistance movements, still in the sway of their former colonizers, these and other (post)colonial nations emerged touting independence. Writers in these countries would—suddenly or gradually—find themselves at the center of novel situations of independence and citizenship (or ongoing contestations for either). But where the authors of the nineteenth century—the Balzacs and Dickenses—unified and gave meaning to their oeuvres, this unity was aligned by Barthes and Foucault with capitalism and individualism: bearing the need for a resistance against the forces of authorship as such. Barthes' assault was not on the writer but on the author as authority, as Gayatri Chakravorty Spivak has pointed out.[40] Yet this new generation of independence authors came to prominence only to be told that, for the sake of interpretation as authors, assigning meaning and unity to their work, they were dead. The wind was blowing in several directions, to and from the author's living presence; other licked forefingers were raised to gauge the applicability of Barthes to the postcolonial author.

It may be exaggeration to say that the pronouncement of the death of the author is necessarily a colonial act, but it is clear that for many anticolonial and postcolonial writers (such, early on, as Said and Glissant), the manifestation of an author's presence and humanity are complementary to anticolonial politics. It follows, then, that even as the death of the author and the play of signification might have served to liberate authorship, textuality, and, indeed, culture and civilization from the sign of "man" who would be "erased, like a face drawn in sand at the edge of the sea" in Foucault's sense, nonetheless such antihumanism seemed (and continues to seem) to anticolonial writers not always to be located in the sphere of emancipatory anticapitalism but rather quite prematurely in the zone of the reactionary and, indeed regressive.[41] To turn to the typewriter or the pen was meant to be a sign of liberation and not one of death.

THE DEATH OF THE AUTHOR AND ANTICOLONIAL THOUGHT

The Death of the Author and Anticolonial Thought represents an attempt to examine key, early efforts by anticolonial authors to analyze and, at times, resist the aesthetic and political consequences of poststructuralist and related ideas about authorship. In spite of the very different histories of dispossession, traditions of self-representation, and decolonizing projects that emerge from postcolonial spaces, the impact of such poststructuralist claims as the death of author, the author function and other related ideas are felt across both terrains, though never in the same way.

In this book, I identify figures who have critiqued colonization using the term anticolonial, acknowledging this term remains a heuristic and resisting the urge to see it as a panacea for questions of nomenclature. Postcolonial, by contrast, as a term seems less an apt designation for Edward Said as a Palestinian intellectual, in spite of his often being yoked with the emergence of this movement in criticism from the latter years of the twentieth century onward. Maurice Jr. Labelle, for instance, has identified the importance of such figures as Fanon to Said in the latter's commitment to decolonization.[42] Yet decolonization itself seems potentially fraught, given its coinage not by writers engaged in decolonial agitation but rather by a European thinker concerned with the socioeconomic management of the loss of Europe's colonies: Moritz Bonn. As Priyamvada Gopal usefully summarizes it according to Bonn's account, as he produced his work at the London School of Economics, often with a sense of Eurocentric focus:

> 'decolonisation' was a term equivalent to the counter-colonisation or '*gegenkolonisation*', a concept which he had developed to describe opposition in Germany to the country's bitter and punitive post-Versailles experience. Over time Bonn would drop this term in favour of 'decolonisation.'[43]

Where decolonization became palatable to theorists associated with a European management of transition to independence, anticolonial as a term arguably has no such history. Even so, if Fanon is a paradigmatic anticolonial thinker, his critique of Empire, colony, and the process of decolonization is as articulated against the emergence of postcolonial elites as it is with European and other transnational exploitation. As Gopal aptly sums it up: "the targets of [Fanon's] critique were often as much both native tyrannies and nationalist elites as they were colonial rulers, just as much indigenous capitalism as foreign firms; the collaboration between these parties was also of relevance."[44] This is a charge leveled at decolonization theory by Fanon the anticolonial thinker, drawing in all the complexity of the process of decolonization in critical and sustained opposition. Anticolonialism then opposes Empire even as it is vigilant about the promises of decolonization. Similarly, Glissant was quite critical of the legacy of decolonization as a process of thought even if much of his work engages with ways of thinking about colonization, Empire, the middle passage and its aftermath as relation vis a vis the whole-world

(*Tout-monde*). For Glissant decolonization was a promise with pitfalls also, principally, as he says in the *Baton Rouge Interviews* conducted with Alexandre Leupin, given his sense that:

> [t]hese struggles of decolonization, which had necessitated so many sacrifices, so many deaths, and so many wars, had been pursued on the very principle that the West had formulated, the principle of identity as a unique root. I didn't hesitate to join in these struggles, but I was beset by misgivings.[45]

As such then, I have tended in this study to think about the anticolonial as a sustained and ongoing resistance to Empire and colonization as a(n) (undoubtedly flawed and limited) means to distinguish it from decolonization and postcoloniality.

To return to intentionalism, then, and its alignment with the anticolonial, one crucial example of an alternative, intentionalist mode of signification to examine is the way black writers—African American, Caribbean, and otherwise—in the new world have established a unique tradition of approaching the relation between meaning and intention. As Henry Louis Gates Jr. documented more than thirty years ago, the African-American tradition of "Signifyin[g]" is a key feature of the way U.S. modes of the sign are infiltrated, parodied, and challenged by and within black modes of expression and meaning-making. As Gates asserts, framing his 1988 study, *The Signifying Monkey*:

> Black texts Signify upon other black texts in the tradition by engaging in what Ellison has defined as implicit formal critiques of language use, of rhetorical strategy. Literary Signification, then, is similar to parody and pastiche, wherein parody corresponds to what I am calling motivated Signification while pastiche would correspond roughly to unmotivated Signification. By motivation I do not mean to suggest the lack of intention, for parody and pastiche imply intention, ranging from severe critique to acknowledgment and placement within a literary tradition.[46]

Black signification, for Gates, can often be viewed, then, not only in intertextual terms in the loose sense we associate with the French theoretical idea—beginning with Julia Kristeva—of a network of signs whose interrelations can be analyzed and interrelated. For Gates, the trope "signifyin'" derives from black vernacular uses of the world, which deploy textual play and satirical meaning-making. For Gates, Signifyin[g] upon other texts and utterances is present, willed, and intentional. Even the word "Signifyin[g]" comes, in this elaboration, to mean a black mode of relating to and (re)occupying signification is given to a significant vernacular practice of sign making and the production of meaning. Allow me to quote Gates at length:

> "Signification," [differs from] the standard English sign, "signification." This level of conceptual difficulty stems from—indeed, seems to have been intentionally inscribed within—the selection of the signifier "Signification" to represent a concept remarkably distinct from that concept represented by the standard English signifier, "signification." For the standard English word is a homonym of the Afro-American vernacular word. And, to compound the dizziness and the giddiness that we must experience in the vertiginous movement between these two "identical" signifiers, these two homonyms have everything to do with each other and, then again, absolutely nothing.[47]

Note not only that Gates, in this precise and thought-provoking parsing of this doubled signifier ("signifyin[g]"), identifies the structural mode by which the sign itself uncannily takes up its powerful place as a black infiltration of "English," but also that he emphasizes its intentional assertion in this cultural space. Signifyin[g] doesn't simply happen without a willful signifier. Gates will elsewhere strikingly express what he means:

> Let me attempt to account for the complexities of this (re)naming ritual, which apparently took place anonymously and unrecorded in antebellum America. Some black genius or a community of witty and sensitive speakers emptied the signifier "signification" of its received concepts and filled this empty signifier with their own concepts. By doing so, by supplanting the received, standard English concept associated by (white) convention with this particular signifier, they (un)wittingly disrupted the nature of the sign = signified/signifier equation itself. I bracket wittingly with a negation precisely because origins are always occasions for speculation. Nevertheless, I tend to think, or I wish to believe, that this guerrilla action occurred *intentionally* on this term, because of the very concept with which it is associated in standard English.[48]

I do not wish only to emphasize the apt doubling of intentionality in Gates' choice to fix his analysis to the very category it will avow. The suggestion is already there in this astounding passage when he characterizes the doer of this "guerrilla" deed. This was no accident of history but something of an intervention, at what stage we know not, by "[s]ome black genius or a community of witty and sensitive speakers" and this individual or community's *intentional* act, operated to remake the vernacular of an entire community and the language of the community that oppressed them in so far as the first would play upon, infiltrate and relate to that oppressive community. The point is not that signs never deanchor from their initial moment of intention but that such jokes, jibes, and "guerilla acts" imply a strategic choice at a particular moment in time and space.

Gates' contributions are profound and also, fortunately, still fairly well recalled in the recent history of literary criticism. The bulk of this book seeks to document the immediate and less well remembered way literary intentionalism was engaged with by black and decolonial writers around the question of such matters as literary intention and what beginning with it (rather than discarding it) might mean. In this chapter of this book I chart the views of key thinkers about colonization and writers such, notably, as Harris and Fanon. While I do not mean to suggest either simplistic continuities between anticolonial thinkers across time and geographies necessarily, I nonetheless find Fanon in particular to anticipate the sense of communal concern that both Glissant and Said will later yolk to poetic intention at its beginnings. The work of Glissant is coming to have a great deal of purchase in the academy, but as I assert in Chapter 2, the emphasis placed on the Glissant of the later "poetics of relation" is thoroughly reliant on underemphasized early work on what he called "poetic intention." I go on to elaborate a reading of Glissant's oeuvre that emphasizes the role of poetic intention and related concepts such as opacity. But as I also emphasize, Glissant's sense of intentionality is as cognisant of the sense of trace and spectrality as any poststructuralist; it is simply the case that Glissant begins with intention in order to note its limits, rather than discarding the category in advance.

In Chapter 3 of this book, I chart a similarly less well-recalled aspect of Said's early writing that takes up intentionalism as a function not only of an alternative aesthetics but of decolonial politics. I track the early influence of poststructuralism on Said (and his resistance to elements of it even then) to his later reactions to the politics of this system of thought in figures such as Foucault and Jean-Francois Lyotard. These paradigmatic early decolonial theorists both read and learned from Barthes, Foucault, and Derrida and also elaborated alternative epistemological, aesthetic, and political understandings of the relation between the literary text and the world it engages with. Yet as my mention of Harris shows, there is an extensive tradition of thinking authorship not in relation to these French thinkers but in a wholly original way. For this reason, my conclusion surveys a number of related contemporary anticolonial intellectuals with an emphasis on the West Indies, beginning by returning to Harris as well as via Barbadian poet and thinker Kamau Brathwaite and Jamaican theorist Sylvia Wynter to name only a few. By drawing from anticolonial constellations such as these, I aim to emphasize a parallel but meaningfully comparable sense of political resistance to reductive ideas about the author's death. In doing so, we find that one key emphasis around the "communal concern" named by Said lies in a sense of storytelling that draws in culture and community—rather than the kind of individualistic author that Barthes was rejecting in the first place.

While not suggesting that the (post)structuralist literature on authorship is necessarily given to dispossession and colonization, I want to assert that an erasure of authorial agency was experienced by anticolonial writers from as early as the immediate years after Barthes' essay to much more recently (due to its continued impact, anthologization, and inclusion in English and Creative Writing syllabi). Similarly, though, it bears repeating that key anticolonial thinkers also explored the limits of intention. Without overly generalizing, the contention of this book is that this is a question of emphasis and narration. Where poststructuralist thinkers narrate the occlusion of authorial presence, anticolonial thinkers begin (to use Said's term) with it. But these same anticolonial thinkers are also sanguine to the complex reorientation of the author through writing and the text's iterable incorporation of this presence. The death of the author, it seems, may have been greatly exaggerated, most of all, in relation to the legacy of colonization and writing against it from the Global South.

NOTES

1. See Anshuman Mondal, "The Self-Transgressions of Salman Rushdie: Re-Reading *The Satanic Verses*" in *Islam and Controversy*. London: Palgrave-Macmillan, 2014, 97–146.
2. Said uses the term affiliation across numerous texts. For a summative accounting of this, see for instance: E. San Juan, Jr., "Edward

Said's Affiliations: Secular Humanism and Marxism," in *Atlantic Studies* 3, 1 (2006): 43–61.
3. See Michael Thorpe, "Risky Deconstruction: The Rushdie Affair," in *World Literature Written in English* 35, 1 (1996): 21–32; Gayatri Chakravorty Spivak, "Reading Salman Rushdie," in *Outside in the Teaching Machine* Routledge, 1993; Mondal.
4. Said *Beginnings: Intention and Method*. London: Granta, 1985 [1975] 13.
5. Zadie Smith, "Rereading Barthes and Nabokov," in *Changing My Mind: Occasional Essays*. New York: Penguin, 2009, 41–56, 43.
6. Matthew Arnold, "The Function of Criticism at the Present Time," in *Lectures and Essays in Criticism*. Ed. R. H. Super, New York: University of Michigan, 1962, 258–284.
7. Arnold, "The Function of Criticism," 270.
8. Derrida, "Signature, Event, Context;" Michel Foucault, "What is an Author," in *The Foucault Reader*, 101–120.
9. Chris Baldick, *Criticism and Literary Theory 1890 to the Present*, London: Routledge, 1996, 124.
10. Baldick *Criticism and Literary Theory 1890 to the present*, 124.
11. Wilson Harris, "Art and Criticism," *Tradition, The Writer and Society*. London: New Beacon Books, 1967, 7, 9.
12. Roland Barthes, "The Death of the Author," in *Image, Music, Text*. London: Fontana, 1977, 143.
13. Smith, "Rereading Barthes and Nabokov," 42.
14. Barthes, "The Death of the Author," 143.
15. Barthes, "The Death of the Author," 142.
16. Barthes, "The Death of the Author," 143.
17. Barthes, "The Death of the Author," 145.
18. Barthes, "The Death of the Author," 147.
19. Barthes, "The Death of the Author," 148.
20. Melissa Lucashenko, "I Pity the Poor Immigrant," in *JASAL* 17, 1 (2017), 1–10, 1.
21. Jeanine Leane, "No Longer Malleable Stuff." In *Overland* 241 (2020).
22. Michel Foucault, "What is an Author," in *The Foucault Reader*, 101–120.
23. Foucault, "What is an Author," 103.
24. Foucault, "What is an Author," 104.
25. Foucault, "What is an Author," 118.

26. Foucault, "What is an Author," 102.
27. Burke, *The Death and Return of the Author: Criticism and Subjectivity in Barthes, Foucault and Derrida*. Edinburgh: Edinburgh University Press, 1992, 20–61.
28. Burke, *The Death and Return of the Author* 47.
29. Burke, *The Death and Return of the Author* 47.
30. Jane Gallop, *The Deaths of the Author: Reading and Writing In Time*. Durham, NC: Duke University Press, 2011.
31. Judith Ryan, *The Novel After Theory*. New York: Columbia University Press, 2011, 25.
32. Aryan Arya, *The Postwar Novel and the Death of the Author*. Cham: Palgrave Macmillan, 2020; Philip Sayers, *Authorship's Wake: Writing After the Death of the Author*. New York: Bloomsbury, 2021.
33. Ryan, *The Novel After Theory*. 50–54.
34. Mark McGurl, *The Program Era: Postwar Fiction and the Rise of Creative Writing*, Harvard University Press, 2009, 20.
35. Timothy Bewes, *Free Indirect: The Novel in a Postfictional Age*, New York: Columbia University Press, 2022, 19.
36. Bewes, *Free Indirect*, 44–45.
37. See Wayne C. Booth, *The Rhetoric of Fiction*. Chicago: The University of Chicago Press, 1961; See Franco Moretti, *Distant Reading*. New York: Verso, 2013.
38. Bewes, *Free Indirect*, 83.
39. Bewes, *Free Indirect*, 83.
40. Spivak, "Reading Salman Rushdie" in *Outside in the Teaching Machine*, 217–218.
41. Michel Foucault, *The Order of Things: An Archeology of the Human Sciences*. New York: Vintage, 1973, 422.
42. Maurice Jr. M Labelle, "On the Decolonial Beginnings of Edward Said," in *Modern Intellectual History* 19, 2 (June 2022): 600–624.
43. Priyamvada Gopal, "On Decolonization and the University," in *Textual Practice* 35, 6 (2021): 873–99, 882.
44. Gopal, "On Decolonization and the University," 882.
45. Édouard Glissant and Alexandre Leupin, *The Baton Rouge Interviews* Trans. Kate M. Cooper. Liverpool: Liverpool University Press, 2020, 30.

46. Henry Louis Gates, Jr. *The Signifying Monkey: A Theory of African-American Literary Criticism*. London: Oxford University Press, 1989, xxvii.
47. Gates, Jr., *The Signifying Monkey: A Theory of African-American Literary Criticism*. London: Oxford University Press, 1989, 2014, 50.
48. Gates, Jr. *The Signifying Monkey: A Theory of African-American Literary Criticism*. London: Oxford University Press, 1989, 2014, 51.

CHAPTER 2

"With the Intention of Opening Up the Future": Decolonial Authorship Before Barthes' Essay

Abstract This chapter takes a step back from the overview of the death of the author premise given in the previous chapter to examine key figures who emphasized the connection between authorial intent and decolonization even prior to Barthes' declaration emphasized the controversies of the various position taking implied by his essay. The chapter emphasizes the work of two figures: Wilson Harris and then, even more significantly, Frantz Fanon. Each of these figures differently explored the meaning of authorial intent and the creative act in conceptualizing the role of the author in anticolonial politics.

Keywords New humanism · Frantz Fanon · Wilson Harris · Decolonization · Third Worldism

Late in the preceding introduction chapter, I remarked that for many anticolonial intellectuals in the mid-twentieth century, the act of writing is a sign of liberation. However, this observation alone, while necessary, is also insufficient. Until we know what writing and its relation to presence means (or meant) to these intellectuals, it remains perhaps insufficient to simply invoke decolonization and humanism—even, as Frantz Fanon called it, a "new humanism"—as a maneuver in and of itself.[1] As Spivak cautions by asking,

> Are we obliged to repeat the argument that, as metropolitan writing is trying to get rid of a subject that has too long been the dominant [the author], the postcolonial writer must still foreground his traffic with the subject position? Too easy, I think. Not because the migrant must still consider the question of identity, plurality, roots. But because fabricating decentered subjects as the sign of the times is not necessarily these times decentering the subject.[2]

For Spivak, context, including "identity, plurality, roots" may be necessary even if they be insufficient to "decentr[e] the subject." Spivak moves quickly here, but one upshot of this quotation seems to clearly be the recognition that the "postcolonial writer" must continue to lean on a subject position that metropolitan intellectuals are "trying to get rid of" for reasons of strategy and tactics, emancipation and resistance. Yet the worry that this position is "too easy" seems to linger. Insisting on a "decentred subject" or indeed, "fabricating" a decentered subject as "sign of the times" can, it would seem to undo or decenter the subject. Spivak's maneuver is heavily compacted and doubled. The migrant who would insist on their whole identity (indeed) intention is, Spivak's claim seems to be, already fragmented along with their intention. But the second of the auxiliary claims made here insist that the subject is not necessarily "decentered" by the death of the author (which I take to be one meaning of these fabricated decentered subjects along with other meanings). What emerges is the fact that while the migrant subject (for example) is always already fragmented, it is not necessarily made any more so by a declaration such as Barthes'.

Isn't one conclusion implied by Spivak's bifurcated query of the death of the author also that the author is more important than ever, though, especially in the postcolony with its textual lineage? If the subject is not decentered by gestures to "identity, plurality, roots," the subject who writes—the author—returns as more present than ever before. If anything, Spivak's statement suggests that it is metropolitan writing *such as* Barthes' that has not decentered what she here calls, "the migrant." In other words, we should avoid assuming that the postcolonial author needs authorship to align to humanism (at least in some crude sense) in order to resist colonization. Indeed, as Anthony C. Alessandrini suggests, if humanism is to be engaged in anticolonial struggles it is not so much so that the former can be applied to the latter but more a question of "how the struggle for decolonization holds the potential to undo the false universalism claimed by this [capital-H Humanism] intellectual structure."³ Alessandrini quotes Fanon in a doubled relation to humanism:

> In its narcissistic monologue the colonialist bourgeoisie, by way of its academics, had implanted in the minds of the colonized that the essential values—meaning Western values—remain eternal in despite all errors attributable to man. The colonized intellectual accepted the cogency of these ideas and there in the back of his mind stood a sentinel on duty guarding the Greco-Roman pedestal. But during the struggle for liberation, when the colonized intellectual touches base again with his people, this artificial sentinel is smashed to smithereens.⁴

For Alessandrini in his reading of Fanon, Europe (again in the words of the latter), "never stops talking of man yet massacres him at every one of its street corners, at every corner of the world."⁵ And what is apparent in Fanon's work, as Alessandrini nicely emphasizes is that a new humanism will be a form dialectically elaborated and turned against the hypocrisy that European humanism has frequently found itself to be in the twentieth and twenty-first centuries. As Alessandrini puts it: "It is also readily apparent from the quote above that Fanon calls on the decolonization movements to carry out this struggle both against European humanism and simultaneously in the name of humanism."⁶ Neil Lazarus has cautioned against either on the one hand eliding Fanon's humanism in favor of a logic of postcolonial (even postmodern) theorizing or on the other, romanticizing Fanon's Third Worldism (and with it his secular socialism) such that one covers over the specific commitments of the Algerian peasantry on whom the Front de Libération Nationale (FLN) for whom he worked.⁷ It is clear enough now to see that what Lazarus calls the "'postcolonial' ideologeme" aimed in part to depoliticize Fanon's contribution, decontextualize it, and partly to deemphasize its recognition of the exigency of violent decolonial resistance in anticolonial struggle. Yet, even the Third Worldist interpretation of Fanon based on FLN praxis fails to acknowledge, Lazarus suggests, that the "Algerian peasantry was never fully committed to the secular, socialist vision projected from the movement" rather retaining a commitment to the precolonial, "Arab, Berber, and Islamic past" as Ian Clegg puts it.⁸ In light of Lazarus' dialectical take on and caveats to Fanon's legacy, the question of Fanon's attitude to artistic practice and authorial presence becomes strangely urgent. This is so because the latter's impact was not only on revolutionary practice from Algiers to the California of Huey P. Newton and the black panthers (for it impacted both these spaces and many in between). Fanon's impact was also in the realm of art and ideas, in turn, informing his revolutionary practice and that of those numerous thinkers, artists, activists, and revolutionaries he has influenced.

But equally still, given this ambivalence to humanism (with the various interpretations of its ideologemes, postcolonial and Third Worldist alike), there emerges an ambiguity with regards to the figure of the author. The figure of the author would seem to be the manifestation of the human in relation to the practice of inscription. To decolonize the author as a figure is to go some way toward rethinking the figure of the human. For instance, we can develop from what Spivak further says, the notion that the death of the author premise cannot be made to decenter the authorial subjectivity of the postcolonial writer. No surprise, then, that authorship as manifest in the paratext and its variants imbues a consistently insurmountable mark on textual scholarship. Nonetheless, as we shall see, anticolonial writers writing even prior to Barthes' essay intuited the pragmatic utility and theoretical potential in beginning with the gambit of intention rather than erasing it in advance.

This short opening chapter, then, aims to zone in on this problematic by examining such figures as Guyanese novelist and essayist Wilson Harris and (especially) Martinican psychoanalyst and revolutionary Frantz Fanon and who each differently elaborated a sense of authorship's relation to culture and community. Fanon's notion of a "new humanism" and its relationship to art, literature, and, in particular, the question of intentionality was not, for Fanon, at all extraneous to the realm of the aesthetic. I want to explore ways these authors aimed to think humanism and authorship without falling into the trap which Spivak referred to as a "too easy" retreat from the complexity of the subject. Not only does Fanon write on these topics prior to Barthes' 1967 declaration and that is another key ambition of this chapter as an opening provocation: That not only did such figures as Glissant and Said respond to Barthes early on but other figures preceding the latter had the question of authorship and its vicissitudes in mind already.

By maneuvering to this preceding moment, I want to suggest that the relation between authorial presence and humanist agency had been considered prior to the Barthesian critique even as the latter event certainly had an impact on anticolonial thought as we shall see in the following chapters. At any rate, questions of humanism and cultural production were already concerns that held currency in anticolonial discussions on literature and the arts. In this way, while the turn represented by Barthes' essay foregrounds a significant one for anticolonial writers (even as something to be resisted or complicated), I begin with some attention to the moment that preceded it. This chronology is vital because, while the impact of the 1967 "death of the author" idea precipitated much reaction and rethinking of authorship, from such figures as Glissant and Said, the articulations of preceding anticolonial writers and thinkers also stressed presence, intention, and authorship—never in an uncomplicated way—even *avant la lettre*, prior to the author's declared death.

In 1951, responding to Georg Lukàcs' notion that "creative work may, and often does have entirely different meanings to what the author hopes," Harris asks, "can the creative artist overcome the changeless spirit and mechanical institutions of his world ruthlessly enforced on him?"—a question that would launch him to a series of aesthetic speculations up to and including 1967, the year of Barthes' essay.[9] Harris, by this later date, chose a path that refused to ever give up on the writer as a creative figure. As he argued in a lecture delivered that year at the University of Edinburgh, "the writer—the 'creative' writer at whom we have been looking—both transcends and undermines (or deepens if you will) the mode of society since the truth of community which he pursues is not a self-evident fact: it is neither purely circumscribed nor purely produced by economic circumstance."[10] Harris would go on to the question of context as he continued, articulating an astute reading of Cold War politics while not surrendering his essential view that creative writers relate as active figures to the society that surrounds them and has yet to be defined ("is not a self-evident fact"). The author, for Harris, remakes the context of his work as much as he is made by it. One key aspect of Harris' later elaboration that I want to underscore is the way the presence of the creative writer is meaningful not only or indeed most importantly through relation to some phenomenological reflective self but to a much greater degree, in relation to "the truth of community" and "the mode of society." Harris would maintain an interest in the relation between authorship and community till even later critical writings. For instance, in 1981's collection *Explorations*, Harris would collect his subsequent examinations of such themes as the relation between tradition and what he had in a 1973 essay called the "subjective imagination." In that essay, he opens by directly asserting that, "it seems to me that the time is ripe now for imaginative writers to speak of their own work—a time when it seems the imagination itself is on trial."[11] The "trial" to which such writers are subjected (for Harris) was derived in large part from the alienation of subjective experience and community connection by technology. "Something," he said, "is seriously wrong with man's imagination when [...] a gulf exists between what appears to be a technological achievement and what is in fact the state of community in which he lives."[12] Writers write for others and this is a crucial point of emphasis for Harris as it will be for Fanon.

Fanon made one of his earliest evocations of a new humanism in 1952's *Black Skin White Masks*, at a moment temporally adjacent to Harris' declarations about authorship. But it would not be until the later *Wretched of the Earth*, published in 1961, that the former would begin to thread together the meaning of humanism and the place of the creative writer in relation to anticolonial struggle. In the earlier of these, Fanon would refer to the prospect of this "new humanism," only once, though early and prominently—with some irony and indeed an almost rhetorical tone. Breaking from prose into an almost verse-based construction, Fanon writes:

> Why am I writing this book? Nobody asked me to. Especially not those for whom it is intended. So? So in all serenity my answer is that there are too many idiots on this earth. And now that I've said it. I have to prove it.
> Striving for a New Humanism.
> Understanding Mankind.
> Our Black Brothers.
> I believe in you, Man.
> Racial Prejudice.
> Understanding and Loving.[13]

Fanon, as he animates himself on the page, seeks to find a proclamation that is made to the measure of his project—to the compass of his suffering, as Cesaire might say—and among these possible proclamations concerns the question of a "New Humanism" fit for both "Mankind" and the reality of blackness, which he will later call its "lived experience."[14] Yet just as is so frequently inherent in the tone of *Black Skin White Masks*, Fanon slips into self questioning almost immediately—examining the idea from all angles in almost a phenomenological performance. This is because the phenomenological dimension of this early work seeks to portray the sense of self questioning and existential dread engendered within the racism experienced by a black man in a white world. Immediately after the evocation of "Understanding and Loving," Fanon moves to this register:

> I'm bombarded from all sides with hundreds of lines that *try* to foist themselves on me. A single line, however, would be enough. All it needs is one simple answer and the black question would lose all relevance.
> What does man want?
> What does the black man want?[15]

In this way, the question of any new humanism is for Fanon precisely that: a question, in this period. And to the degree that *Black Skin White Masks* poses it (necessarily) in relation to race—to the lived experience of the black subject as it pertains to the morass of doubt and victimization that the black individual was then and is now to be subordinated—the substantive definition of a new humanism remains in a state of suspension and deferral. Where the earlier Fanon explores this imposition of racial subordination on the question of humanism, the later Fanon seeks, I suggest, to solve this condition by reference to anticolonial struggle and, with a particular focus on the question of national culture.

In the chapter of *The Wretched of the Earth* titled "On National Culture"—originally presented at the Second Congress of Black Artists and Writers in Rome in 1959—Fanon would reorient and expand the meaning of humanism in relation to art, culture, and their national instantiations. He would take a rhetorical conjecture: new humanism with a question mark (from *Black Skin White Maska*) and reconstruct it entirely through a sustained account of anticolonial humanist theory and practice. In his address, Fanon rejects such attitudes as Negritude and pan-Africanism for collapsing the specific conditions of struggle differently experienced by varying colonized and (his focus in particular here), African people. But he does so in order to impose a more meaningful cross-cultural relation dialectically in the form of an evocation of the international. As Fanon puts it:

> Negritude thus comes up against its first limitation, namely, those phenomena that take into account the historicizing of men. "Negro" or "Negro-African" culture broke up because the men who set out to embody

it realized that every culture is first and foremost national, and that the problems for which Richard Wright or Langston Hughes had to be on the alert were fundamentally different from those faced by Léopold Senghor or Jomo Kenyatta.[16]

Throughout Fanon's address, this question of national culture comes to center related questions of art, literature, and the figure of the storyteller. Fanon will close his discourse (that is to become this section of his later book), by emphasizing the way the determination of national culture is a condition of the emergence of a more universal cross-cultural elaboration. The chapter closes with these lines:

> Far then from distancing it from other nations, it is the national liberation that puts the nation on the stage of history. It is at the heart of national consciousness that international consciousness establishes itself and thrives. And this dual emergence, in fact, is the unique focus of all culture.[17]

In other words, Fanon is not rejecting the ambition for a pan-African or otherwise international discourse but rather emphasizing the need for "national culture" to emerge within particular concrete situations on home terrain, prior to any possible internationalism to come. In this way there emerges a dialectic between national culture and new humanism in his work and this tension relies upon a concrete sense of the author, creator, and storyteller as having a relationship with the community, national or otherwise, that they set out to represent. This is crucial to note, given that a common thread we will find running through anticolonial thought on authorship whether before the declaration of the death of the author or after invests heavily in the notion of speaking for and in relation to a group or a people.

Fanon is quite precise in his particular vision of the struggle of a writer to relate the story of a people. He elaborates "three stages" in the form of works of art produced by colonized intellectuals:

> First, the colonized intellectual proves he has assimilated the colonizer's culture. His works correspond point by point with those of his metropolitan counterparts. The inspiration is European and his works can be easily linked to a well-defined trend in metropolitan literature.[18]

This imitative stage of relating to the colonizer's culture in an attempt to become an equal is, however, to be overcome, for Fanon, in two further stages.

> In a second stage, the colonized writer has his convictions shaken and decides to cast his mind back. [. . .] the colonized writer is not integrated with his people, since he maintains an outsider's relationship to them, he is content to remember. Old childhood memories will surface, old legends be reinterpreted on the basis of a borrowed aesthetic, and a concept of the world discovered under other skies. [. . .] Finally, a third stage, a combat stage where colonized writer, after having tried to lose himself among the people, with the people, will rouse the people. Instead of letting the people's lethargy prevail, he turns into a galvanizer of the people. Combat literature, revolutionary literature, national literature emerges.[19]

In this way, the wider dialectic between national and international culture is preceded by a similar kind of stage-based precession from fetishism for the colonial through the nostalgic relation described as the second stage toward a willed engagement with the intellectual's people and nation. In this way, for Fanon, the writer and the intellectual has, necessarily to engage with the people they seek to represent in the process of writing.

The question that remains to be asked is: How does this self-consciously revolutionary literary praxis relate to intentionalism within literature? There is, as it turns out, a crucial but easily missed rhetoric of intention employed by Fanon at key moments. For instance, as he continues to define the sensibility of the writer of national culture, he explicitly refers to the intention of this writer: "[w]hen the colonized intellectual writing for his people uses the past he must do so with the *intention* of opening up the future, of spurring them into action and fostering hope."[20] This is not an orientation to the event given through the sign or the text, but rather an insistence on the willful capacity of the subject to act. Fanon's emphasis is on the sensibility of the writer as they relate to political action and community formation. He seeks to narrate an attitude attuned to action that does not determine the text *tout court* perhaps but will nonetheless inevitably impact it.

Of course, as Fanon notes, success is not guaranteed and the attitude can be miscalculated or misguided: a "colonized poet who is concerned with creating a work of national significance, who insists on describing his people, misses his mark" if and where he refuses to make concessions of his own flesh and blood, of his self to those others to whom his work is dedicated (to paraphrase the lines of Haitian poet René Depestre that Fanon uses to make his point).[21] Revolutionary poetry, speaking for a people, is a project and not a *fait accompli*. Nonetheless, for Fanon, "the first duty of the colonized poet is to clearly define the people, the subject of his creation."[22] The colonized poet must have an explicit conception of who this people is for whom they, the poet, writes.

In any case it is through relation to the intentional act of the writer that not only revolutionary action is understood by Fanon to take place, it is also the locus of the emergence of new humanism in its more fully profound sense. Fanon frames it in this way:

> This struggle, which aims at a fundamental redistribution of relations between men, cannot leave intact either the form or substance of the people's culture. After the struggle is over, there is not only the demise of colonialism, but also the demise of the colonized. This new humanity, for itself and for others, inevitably defines a new humanism. This new humanism is written into the objectives and methods of the struggle. A struggle, which mobilizes every level of society, which expresses the intentions and expectations of the people, and which is not afraid to rely on their support almost entirely, will invariably triumph.[23]

In this way, through national culture, Fanon dialectically realigns the struggle for a widely embracing new humanism to the intentional program of the individual artist and in their relation to collective struggle. And while it is not the case that the intentions of creative writers are necessarily to align with the struggle of a people—an anticolonial struggle for instance, it perhaps is the case (and it is certainly Fanon's assertion) that they nonetheless have tremendous power in their alignment with the struggle against colonial domination. As we shall see in the chapters to follow, it was a struggle to unpack and sustain the sensibility of an alignment between the writer and the people that was maintained in the work of Glissant and Said (with caveats in either case).

NOTES

1. Frantz Fanon, *Black Skin, White Masks*. Trans. Richard Philcox New York Grove Press, 2008, xi.

2. Spivak, "Reading Salman Rushdie," in *Outside in the Teaching Machine* Routledge, 1993, 225.
3. Anthony C. Alessandrini. *Frantz Fanon and the Future of Cultural Politics: Finding Something Different*. London: Lexington Books, 2014, 52.
4. Fanon, *The Wretched of the Earth*. Trans. Richard Philcox. New York: Grove Press, 2004, 10–11, cited in Alessandrini, *Frantz Fanon and the Future of Cultural Politics*, 52.
5. Cited in Alessandrini, *Frantz Fanon and the Future of Cultural Politics*, 52.
6. Alessandrini, *Frantz Fanon and the Future of Cultural Politics*, 53.
7. Neil Lazarus, *The Postcolonial Unconscious*. Cambridge: Cambridge University Press, 2011, 161–182, esp. 163.
8. Lazarus, *The Postcolonial Unconscious*, 178; Ian Clegg, cited in Lazarus, *The Postcolonial Unconscious*, 179.
9. Wilson Harris, "Art and Criticism," *Tradition, The Writer and Society*. London: New Beacon Books, 1967, 7, 9.
10. Harris, "The Writer and Society," *Tradition, The Writer and Society*, 60.
11. Harris, "A Talk on the Subjective Imagination," *Explorations*. Mundelstrup: Dangaroo Press, 1981, 57.
12. Harris, "A Talk on the Subjective Imagination," 57.
13. Fanon, *Black Skin, White Masks*. Trans. Richard Philcox. New York: Grove Press, 2008, xi.
14. Aimé Césaire, *Notebook of a Return to the Native Land*. Trans. Clayton Eshleman. Middletown: Wesleyan University Press, 2001, 43.
15. Fanon, *Black Skin, White Masks*, xii.
16. Fanon, *The Wretched of the Earth*. Trans. Richard Philcox. New York: Grove Press, 2004, 154.
17. Fanon, *The Wretched of the Earth*, 180.
18. Fanon, *The Wretched of the Earth*, 158.
19. Fanon, *The Wretched of the Earth*, 159.
20. Fanon, *The Wretched of the Earth*, 167. Emphasis added.
21. Fanon, *The Wretched of the Earth*, 162.
22. Fanon, *The Wretched of the Earth*, 163.
23. Fanon, *The Wretched of the Earth*, 178.

CHAPTER 3

The Ghost of the Writer: Édouard Glissant's Poetics of the Whole-World

Abstract This chapter departs from the observation that to understand Édouard Glissant's intervention into literary criticism and poetics it is necessary to contextualize his later work on the poetics of relation adjacent to earlier work on the notion of "poetic intention" which was written around the time of Barthes' essay and shortly afterwards. The chapter then moves to a wide ranging exploration of Glissant's work beginning from this premise examining poetic intention, relation, opacity, and less often considered connections such as Glissant's alignment with other transnational black writers as Léopold Sédar Senghor and Frantz Fanon. From the former he develops a theory of ideas of creolized orality and from the latter he develops his political valence. The chapter explores Glissant as a figure with a complex history that both draws on, resists, and rethinks the tents of poststructuralist theorizations of language.

Keywords Édouard Glissant · Poetics of relation · Poetic intention · Créolité · Léopold Sédar Senghor · Frantz Fanon · Authorship

> Intention perfects itself in Relation.[1]
> —Édouard Glissant

Since his death in 2011, much attention has been paid to the work of Édouard Glissant in the arena of Caribbean studies and of postcolonial studies, and much of this attention—particularly within the latter—has (arguably) focused on Glissant's later political and aesthetic theory, vested in the concept of relation as well as the category of the tout-monde. A palpable afterlife to an author, after that author's death, to be sure. While this recent work recognizes the profound linguistic complexity of this political theory of difference, Glissant's key early concept of "poetic intention" is often glossed and elided in favor of an emphasis on those of his concepts that are more amenable to the received (post)structuralist wisdom surrounding language: the emphasis on the death of the author, the autonomy of the work, and the no doubt rich and evocative necessity of an emphasis on difference (or, indeed, *différance*).[2] Only a few scholars such as, for instance, Michael Wiedorn engage with Glissant's relation to authorship, depicting him as Foucault's "universal intellectual"—not only an author but a vector through which significant ideas are disseminated.[3]

Glissant's training with ethnographer Michel Leiris at the *Musee de L'Homme* in the 1940s bears out his connection to French structuralist experimentation.[4] Still, the not-so-subtle evocation I have made once again of the, perhaps, three key figures in French theoretical disavowals of intention as a meaningful category of literary interrogation, Barthes, Foucault, and Derrida, is of course not accidental. In the introduction of this book, I began by contextualizing the concept of the death of the author, and of the primacy of the author function and I suggested that these categories have been historically privileged to the detriment of a more robust analysis of intention and its doubles perhaps since Wimsatt and Beardsley's work in the 1940s and certainly since Barthes' 1967 declaration. But I mention once again the Francophone (post)structuralist milieu in particular and deliberately in order to emphasize the simultaneous relation and difference between this tradition and Glissant's work. Further, as we shall see, there exist key parallels (as well as differences) between Glissant's work in the space of intention and Glissant's understanding of the politics of black life. The history of a people turns out for Glissant to tell us a great deal about the status of the idea of authorship within that history.

Here I will propose that an analysis of the category of intention might serve as a key prism through which to position Glissant's unique contribution, throughout his career, from his publication of *Poetic Intention* within two years of Barthes' essay to even his most recent contributions. As the epigraph from Glissant that opens this book (taken from a 2006 keynote address) suggests, "intention" remains central to Glissant's elaboration of the rightly recognized ideas of difference and relation: "intention," he says there, brings about a relation to "the whole-world."[5] But what precisely does it mean for Glissant to bind intention to the recognition of difference and relation?[6] If, for those thinkers bound to the poststructuralist emphasis on difference (Gilles Deleuze, Derrida), the trace (Derrida), and discourse (Foucault), the idea of intention in art and literature is for the most part an illusory phantom "presence" obscuring the more salient play of signification and its vicissitudes, then it would seem perverse (at least from an orthodox poststructuralist perspective) for Glissant to tie intention to relation and difference. Yet Glissant developed a theory of the grammar of difference as it relates to artistic and literary intention. As we shall see in Chapter 2, another figure of colonial heritage, Edward Said learned from, adapted, and gradually shed layers of the poststructuralist play of language (without totally extricating himself from its influence). Glissant, in exploring "poetic intention," developed a related lexicon and a grammar for unpacking poetic intention's effect on relation.

A genealogy of the development of relation through intention in Glissant's work does not imply a naïve move but precisely thickens and deepens the recognition of the play of discourse and difference emphasized by such figures as Foucault and Derrida and allows us to compare his project for undertaking this theorization with related early detractors of the death of the author hypothesis, such as Said. By historicizing the condition of colonial dispossession and the linguistic experience of Martinican Creole in particular, Glissant insists upon the necessity of a certain strategic avowal of intentionality with its self-conscious particularity: what he names and develops as "opacity," beginning early in his career. Opacity comes to stand, in *Poetics of Relation,* for an irreducibility of terms in a relation of difference.[7] This irreducibility, Glissant insists, must be retained as a right, even in the face of the embrace of and exchange between positions in a relation of difference. Opacity, amidst all else, stands for the maintenance of a line of division which refuses to relation the right to govern the fate of signification by the Occidental other. In resisting this, Glissant argues that intention and its conscious resistance to colonial linguistic hierarchies is the initial move in navigating the ethical recognition of difference. As such, Glissant's theoretical abstraction from the concrete Martinican experience of colonization develops across his oeuvre to critique too-ready avowals of linguistic and discursive play even as a difference undergirded by relation represents the outcome of his intellectual itinerary. Indeed, without opacity, one has misunderstood relation—in its attenuation to the concrete historicity of the collectivities who would embrace it. And, without attention to the concept of intention, one cannot quite grasp the itinerary of how Glissant narrates relation *alongside* the right to opacity.

Recognizing the difficulty of orienting the role of the author through intention, Glissant is nonetheless less comfortable abandoning these figures than his French contemporaries, and this discomfort, I would assert, tells us much about the desire to retain the category of poetic intention as a touchstone of the agency that an author might metonymically take up for a colonized or (post)colonial community.

Glissant (and, differently, Said) retain the agential possibility that there remains a relation between intention and structure. Indeed, for both, we might say, the specter of intention activates the play of signification, while nonetheless not serving as a naïve guarantor of the willful mastery of author over text. For Said, the presence of intention provides an assertion and an act of expression.

But where Glissant and Said share much in common is in the differentiation of what the latter calls the beginnings (or, what Glissant will call *commencement*) that can be differentiated from absolute conceptions of origin. This is the case for Glissant from the earliest pages of *Poetics of Relation* when he examines the status of the open boat as simultaneously a "womb" giving birth to new lives and modes of life and an "abyss" proffered in the middle passage.[8] Glissant continues by coining the notion of the alluvial—a sediment, stirred in water—as a metaphor for this emergence from the passage across the sea itself. As he puts it at length,

> Experience of the abyss lies inside and outside the abyss. The torment of those who never escaped it: straight from the belly of the slave ship into the violet belly of the ocean depths they went. But their ordeal did not die; it quickened into this continuous / discontinuous thing: the panic of the new land, the haunting of the former land, finally the alliance with the imposed land, suffered and redeemed. The unconscious memory of the abyss served as the alluvium for these metamorphoses.[9]

Here alluvium comes to stand as a signifier for a beginning in the sea which is severed from an earlier origin—sand stirred up on the ocean floor. But Glissant also posits this as a memory of loss and rebirth in the subject of exile (as opposed to errantry, another category of journey which he emphasizes. John E. Drabinski summarizes the sensibility of "abyss" from which the alluvial arises.

> The site or non- site of loss is crucial here. With opacity, Glissant is able to begin a long story about how beginning *after* the Middle Passage, this loss become an abyssal beginning that asserts itself *without reference to what precedes*. Reactivation therefore ceases to structure and regulate notions of remembering and forgetting. This assertion, the first sense of opacity, gives shape to the plantation- birth of Caribbean memory, history, and subjectivity. Abyssal beginning [. . .] is opaque because it begins in the abyss [. . .] an originary opacity that gives the future after arrival and out of catastrophic loss. *A shoreline thinking*.[10]

Crucially, Drabinski ties each stage of this sense of memory of the abyss and beginning after it to the opacity that subsists at every stage, whether the originary opacity that occludes origin (the sea that is history as Derek Walcott would put it and the abyssal rupture of the boat, as Glissant himself would) or the defiant opacity that folds on the black beach among those Caribbean subjects who still retain a trace of that emergent displacement's sense of loss.

For Glissant, expression remains similarly crucial and indeed both give accounts of the distinction between oral and written text across cultures and time periods. While Derrida's famous critique of autoaffection, logocentrism, and the metaphysics of presence takes voice as its key locus, he does so principally as a response to the particular philosophical trajectory through which the logocentric itinerary unfolds, from Plato to Saussure, via Rousseau.[11] But, for Glissant, writing the intersecting communities of black and Caribbean life necessitates not so much a disavowal of writing as the respective limits of individual writing, on the one hand, and oral (particularly Creole) cultures on the other. Rather, Glissant's project consists in imagining the future possibilities promised by an enweaving of the strengths of either medium in producing an agential logic that nonetheless reflects the intersecting communities of the Black Atlantic and the globalizing world more broadly.[12] Against the colonizing universalism of the West, "that self-exportation that nearly always generates a sort of vocation for the universal," Glissant asserts not universalism but relation.[13] What remains to be acknowledged is Glissant's insistence that such a thought of relatedness must begin with the concrete experience of language, just as this concreteness cannot disavow the role of intention in the play of difference and relation (however spectral the trace of intentionality may be). "The writer [*L'écrivain*]," Glissant notes, "is always the ghost of the writer he wants to be."[14]

Poetic Intention after the "Death of the Author"

Glissant's 1990 *Poetics of Relation* connects literary structuralism—wherein "the creator is effaced, or, rather, is done away with, to be revealed in the texture of his creation"—with an unconscious retention of metropolitan French literature. Glissant is certainly respectful of the accomplishments of poststructuralist thought—indeed, he writes famously in the late work of his own relation to the thought of the rhizome in Deleuze and Guattari's work.[15] For instance, he ties the absolute rule of structure to its capacity to unseat "any thought claiming falsely to be final" even as he notes that this tradition retains a Eurocentrism that leaves worldwide geographical and cultural relation "unnoticed, or rather evaded."[16] In later writings such as this, I would contend that Glissant, while praising poststructuralist thought for its critique of the "final," remains critical of the tendency of that thought to eschew the legacy of colonization and the asymmetrical effects of official languages in the geopolitical distribution of the sensible worldwide.[17] For Glissant, the problems of geopolitics are localized principally in the French reduction of Martinican ambitions of decolonization to departmentalization (the self-government of the colony as an overseas "Departement de France"). As he says:

> Departmentalization in 1946: The most concrete form of fear and self-denial, marking the extreme edge of alienation, the limit of self-expression as well. At the same time, other former colonies rejected the Other, setting out on the tough journey towards national identity and independence. (Which does not mean that the problems of neocolonialism were solved.)[18]

It is worth noting that Glissant's criticism of departmentalization is not limited to geopolitics, rather the former is enweaved in the aesthetic: the "limit of self-expression" for Martinican subjects, their alienation of consciousness. Further, Glissant was a leading figure in the Antillo-Guyanese Front in the early 1960s, agitating for independence for overseas French departments.

Glissant had strongly emphasized the role of poetic intention—in beginning a text and not in finalizing its dimensions—from as early as *Poetic Intention* and the essays that make it up.[19] In that work, two years after Barthes had declared the "death" of that most "modern figure," the author, Glissant ties the emergence of relation precisely to the consciousness of a highly proximate figure to that whose post-mortem Barthes had performed: poetic intention.[20] Yet, since the reference points of each writer are so close—Mallarmé and Proust for instance—it is useful to track the degree to which Glissant's conclusions subtly imply an itinerary significantly divergent from Barthes' own. This difference arises in Glissant's attention to the historical condition of the colonized. Barthes contrasts the perplexing fetish of authorial genius with the "mediator, shaman, or speaker" in what he refers to as "ethnographic societies."[21] Barthes' distinction is a diachronic one whereby the genius ascribed to the author function in modernity differs from this figure whose "performance—the mastery of the narrative code— may be admired, but never his 'genius.'"[22] For Barthes, the shamanic figure is simultaneously given a sense of reverence even as he is relegated to a position of absolute difference, whereas for Glissant the figure of the storyteller, shaman, and *quimboiseur* (like the recurring character of his novels, Papa Longoué) is sustained into the present, albeit in relation to the writer and chronicler (located, for instance, in the novels, in Mathieu Béluse, or metatextually, in Glissant himself). Further, for Glissant, the relation between orality (and Creole in particular) and the written is not a diachronic contrast but a synchronic, cross-cultural operation of relation between colony and metropole, across the multiple peripheries of the Caribbean and, indeed, beyond.

Yet Glissant also figures the name (including his own) as something to be erased in the process of writing and of storytelling more broadly. Within Glissant's novel *The Fourth Century (Le Quatrième Siècle*, at a key juncture, the name Glissant is shown to be the reversal of a name bestowed on an emancipated slave, the name of his slave master, Senglis. In the novel, for which Glissant draws on a strong sense of Martinique's colonial history, after 1848 and the emancipation of slaves in colonies of the French Republic, names were issued along with citizenship to the newly freed subjects of France. While many Maroons fought to retain pre-existing names, many others found themselves with "names borne by people from their own region of France, some corner or Bigorre or Poitou: Clarac or Lemesle (playing a good joke on their neighbours back home)," and then, when these names dried up, the colonials "resorted to asking their clients and would even go along with their taking local names: the names of plantations or neighborhoods."[23] Glissant continues, metaleptically breaking the frame by implicating himself, his lineage, and his family in this process of naming as being dominated, robbed of identity, and reborn once more since the encounter with the open boat:

> When impudence became too obvious they amused themselves by turning their names by turning their names around so that at least they would be farther from their origins. Senglis, for example, resulted in Glissant and someone from Courbaril would be named Barricou.[24]

The reversal of names, with Glissant self-deprecatingly implicating himself as the victim by descent and colonial naming after the reversal of the more odious of the plantation owners in the text, seems to suggest the degree to which the author himself is vulnerable to the vicissitudes of slavery's history as much as Mathieu Béluse and Papa Longoué, his storytellers.

As Wiedorn notes, this is discussed in his theoretical writings too, notably *Treatise of the Tout-Monde*. Wiedorn notes that:

> while Glissant's works have often broken identity (*quête identitaire*) by setting in motion a quest for non-origins, or for origins that are ceaselessly deferred [. . .] they have also showcased the author's dabbling in a search for the origins of his own surname. Senglis, a slave owner in the Antilles, surfaces from time to time otherwise, personifying the author's reflections that his own name might be as transformation of the surname Senglis.[25]

Indeed, the *Fourth Century*, the politics of naming punctuates numerous key moments including the metaleptic reference to the implied author, but also in and through the sequence of references to the naming of key black characters. The insistence on resisting renaming is marked at key points by Papa Longoué: "their names were something they set store by. They were perfectly willing for you to have a name provided they gave it to you."[26] And Mathieu learns he has much to struggle against in the history of his name, with Béluse (denoting "well used") reflecting a cruel interpretation that his forebears were pliable and easy to enslave. Reflections of the process of naming on the plantation both before and after emancipation in *The Fourth Century* emphasize Glissant's sense of the power of the name to mark subject through history in a way that is not insignificantly marked by a reference to his own name as author—Senglis branding Glissant indelibly—a mise en abyme, a metaleptic breaking of frames indexing the implied author both inextricably linked to the text and absent from it; the ghost of the writer he wants to be.

As I have just suggested, Glissant both departs from and returns to the question of the author's structural absence (as well as their indelible presence). Despite diverging structural treatment, Barthes' narrative of the emergence and force of the author does have much in common with Glissant's treatment of authorial presence: namely in the emphasis given by each to the status of the human as a property-bearing subject. It is as if each is narrating from another direction, but perhaps finding the same ground as it appears from another angle. Barthes departs from the death of the author, Glissant from a poetic intention that itself gradually vanishes and is erased: the writer [*ecrivain*] always being the ghost of the author, vanishing in advance. For Barthes, the hegemony of the author cannot be disentangled from a status entailed as "the result of capitalist ideology, which has accorded the greatest importance to the author's 'person.'"[27] Glissant similarly locates the function of the author, in its Western instantiation, in the rise of personhood with its double-edged sword of dignity and legal protection alongside the blurring of this concept of autonomy with the rise of the modern institution of private property. As Glissant writes in *Caribbean Discourse*, "[t]he poetically unsayable seems to me tied, in the West, to what one calls the dignity of the human being, in turn surpassed since the historical appearance of private property."[28] Yet, while each writer locates the status of the writing subject in the autonomy afforded the human by enlightenment discourse (from Locke onward and arguably before), for Glissant, this shift is not merely accounted for in a teleological or dialectical move toward the simultaneous reign and expiry of the author, as it is for Barthes.[29] For Glissant, the inextricability of writing from property and the human must be understood as enweaved in the postcolonial condition of those who underwent the period of this development in a condition to which autonomy was denied precisely on the basis of their status as property: the African slaves of the transatlantic slave trade most of all. For

Glissant, the self of the Caribbean writer (and we might add, the post-colonial writer more generally) cannot be understood except by relation to, first, the oral tradition from which he arises (at least in part) and, second, his relation to the Occidental other whose privileged autonomy is guaranteed by the account of language Glissant aims to displace and challenge.

Glissant's continued emphasis on poetic intention might be seen as placing him in the tradition of a Fanonian attention to lived experience, even as his concept of relation bears comparison to poststructuralist suspicion of the enlightenment itinerary of the human and demarcates Glissant from any simplistic humanism.[30] Glissant does not attempt to merely include intention within the play of discourse, nor, when it slips away, to relegate its obscurity to the unconscious of the writing subject. Instead, he offers a taxonomic sketch of the role intention makes as a mark (or signature, as Derrida would have it) on an oeuvre, indeed, in dialogue with a community. As early as *Poetic Intention*, Glissant begins to develop a theory of the author's relation to the work, the community, and the world that resonates with Barthes and Foucault on the one hand, and shares much with Said on the other.[31] As a result, Glissant's view of the cross-cultural develops as a nuanced account of the relation of the writer to both his own community and that of the colonizer that excludes him, while also proffering conjectures on the place this nexus of relations may come to possess in the future.

For Glissant, the conscious or "explicit" intention of an author is inevitably lost in the process of writing and what unconsciously emerges from this failure is, he argues, the imprint of a collective lived experience. As he puts it:

> It would seem in effect that certain oeuvres suffice in themselves, because they assume in their principle that the realized intention will open onto a given that will not be an (other) hidden purpose of the author [*auteur*], but the manifested experience of a people.[32]

For Glissant, then, this sense of authorial purposiveness is manifest only through the imprint of "a people." Glissant continues with a cursory taxonomy of works that speak for regions and spaces, from Dante to Faulkner to Walcott:

These oeuvres break the circle: "author's explicit intention — reality of the work — author's unrealized hidden intention" and distribute it thus: "author's (explicit or non-explicit) intention — reality of the work — (manifested) intention [*extension*] of a people."[33]

Yet, even as Glissant locates the effect of intention not in the author subject but in its expansion into a community, this will not lead to an anti-deconstructive avowal of the full plenitude of speech. Indeed, Glissant seems to suggest that what emerges in the grappling toward conscious mastery of the work (and the inevitable excess that leads this effort to fail) is the linguistic pattern of a concrete and local community. As his dictional choice between intention and *extension* shows, the imprint of the mark of the people *extends* (rather than constrains) the intention of the author, even as the latter's "conscious or unconscious" imprint may indeed remain unrealized. Late in his life and career, when interviewed by Alexandre Leupin, Glissant would in some ways directly clarify his sense of the writer's relation to the community. There he asserts a resistance to the idea that the writer works to incite political action or writes for one or other movement. For Glissant writing for one community is necessarily writing in relation to all, globally. As he says there:

> the reality of writing is to try to reveal these structuring vectors, which concern relations between cultures just as much as the definition of the cultures themselves. If we didn't do one together with the other, it seems to me we would be missing the mark. A great many writers of the countries of the South have undergone these upheavals.[34]

Much of Glissant's meditation on this communal aspect of the individual writer's experience is played out through the imprint of Creole on the Caribbean writer expressing himself or herself through French. Yet Glissant's Caribbean, with its privileged experience of transit, movement, and relation that produces this Creole, will not be labeled as utopian.

Creole, for all its experience of relation, does not emerge in Glissant's work as simply a perfected realization of the intention manifest as relation, but rather as an essential strategy in the opening onto the prospect of such relation manifest as an equal encounter of different linguistic worlds. Creole is only one, historically impacted, instance of the relation between cultures whose full promise must be held out in relation to an uncertain future. Relation—between cultures, between the written and oral, as well as between each link in the chain that leads the author's unrealized intention as a manifestation of her or his particular "people"—emerges as the possible force for cultivating an intention that would manifest not only a people but an other-humanism and an other-globalization. What remains to ask is how this humanism differs from the particular Western form of humanism grounded in the property-holding economic individual. It is not in Creole, nor in Western humanism but in the gap between Creolité and the colonizing force of individual humanism that Glissant locates the emergence or potentiality for an intention realized paradoxically through relation between subjects and cultures. As he puts it, moving cryptically and poetically through the 1969 work, "[i]ntention perfects itself in Relation."[35] How does Glissant arrive at relation through intention in order to better describe the natural process of an increasing globalization of intention as the manifestation of cross-cultural logics? Through an account of the particularly Caribbean and Martinican impasses of the oral and the written, Creole and French, Glissant develops a model for worldliness (though not a universalism) that begins with the particular and opens onto cross-cultural relation, a worldliness not of one experience (whether of colonizer or of colonized) but emergent from the intersection of the diverse and the multiple. It is to this elaboration that I now turn.

Opacity, the Unsayable, and the Vow of the Other

There is a question I have left in abeyance thus far. It is a question opened by the slippage I have allowed to pervade between Barthes' tying of the author to the human, the modern and to capital and Glissant's slightly different move to tie intentionality (along with its historical embedding in the discourse of property) not only to the human but also to the category of the "unsayable." Uncharacteristically avoiding his tendency to *éparter la bourgeoisie* (at least arguably) to the degree that would be taken up vis à vis the author by Barthes and Foucault, Derrida admits in his perhaps most vehement critique of the category of intentionality and the logocentrism of presence and voice: "[i]n this typology, the category of intention will not disappear; it will have its place, but from this place it will no longer be able to govern the entire scene and the entire system of utterances."[36] This remark of Derrida comes in the context of his deconstruction of J. L. Austin's theory of the performative speech act. In insisting on the way speech and particularly performative (and predominantly oral) utterances are always given to the undecidability that is so often attributed to writing alone, Derrida unseats the privileged role attributed to intention in so many Western philosophical systems. For Derrida, speech, just as writing, is given to the possibility of quotation and repetition, "citation and iterability," as much as is the supposed supplemental system of notation we call writing.[37] It is not that, as is often wrongly supposed, Derrida privileges writing over speech but that he emplaces *both* written and oral sign systems within the play of *différance*$_2$ of trace and iterability, that is ascribed in Western philosophy and linguistics—from Plato to Austin—to writing alone.

However, another battle has been fought by postcolonial writers and critics, one that, while not so much critical of the deconstructive project, often appears to be at odds with it. This is at the heart of the battle fought by so many indigenous and diasporic postcolonial thinkers and writers to have credence paid to the complexity of the oral traditions from which they often emerge. Multiple instances could be cited. To recall one particular theory of signification from the black tradition Glissant both emerges and departs from—namely Négritude—one could cite, for instance, the insistence on the ontology of rhythm in Léopold Sédar Senghor's thought. Senghor's theory of "rhythm" as the ontological force that pervades human and particularly *"Négro-Africain"* cultural practices is not merely (or, at least, not only) an essentialism opposed to the Hellenic logic of mimesis, as Souleymane Bachir Diagne has shown.[38] One key thread in Senghor's thought as it concerns the ontology of rhythm is a theory of the sign that, while (I argue) consonant with Derrida's thought of trace and *différance*, emerges less from a sense of the play of signifiers than from the antithetical play of signifieds: of sounds and their conceptual correlates. As Senghor put it in a 1969 speech:

> Black art, therefore, as opposed to Greek art, schematizes, outlines, in a word, stylizes. Through the image, above all, through rhythm. The image born from the force of suggestion of the sign employed: the signifier (*signifiant*). Because the image here is not an image-equation, but an image-analogy, where the word suggests a lot more than it says. The tour de force is all the more eased since Negro-African languages are concrete languages, by which all words, by their root, are as though surrounded by charged images which are, in a sense, concrete and emotional at the same time. Beyond the signifier, the Negro-African voice, precisely senses the signified (*signifié*). Surreality underlies reality. So therefore, the surrealism, better, the Negro-African sub-realism (*sous realism*) is not empirical as that

of the Occident but mystical, metaphysical, participating in a vitalism of symbolism.[39]

It is important to recall of the signifier/signified relation what Senghor implicitly grounds his elaboration upon: the fact that, for Saussure, the signified (*signifié*) is not the referential object for which it is often mistaken, but the representation of voice in the mind. Senghor is not, then, referring to an essentialism of signification's relation to reference, but precisely the opposite: emphasizing instead the vital rhythm of the signified as it informs and conditions the work of the signifier. Is this not precisely an analogy with play? If the "Hellenic" conception of reason that he opposed from as early as the essay "Ce Que L'Homme Noir Apporte" relied on the correspondence between signifier and referent, with the signified only taking on a docile, mediating role, is not the opposite implied here?[40] Here, in opposition to the logic of correspondent signification in which the outside—of meaning, of semantics as reference—plays an active role, instead the phonemic rhythm of enunciation conditions the semantics of expression as much as reference itself. Thus, in emphasizing the emotional and mimetic capacity of the signified to modulate the relation between signifier and referent (beyond merely mediating their relation), Senghor emphasizes the degree to which the play of sound, of signification, of the phoneme qua phoneme, that precedes and conditions signification is not merely a medium but also an active force in the production of meaning. This is not a naïve avowal of the auto-affective voice of the kind deconstructed by Derrida; quite the opposite. In taking on the play of signification that arises in the rhythmic movement of phonemic signifieds, Senghor gestures to the way voice itself is structured through a certain architecture of trace and iterability that cannot be relegated merely to a position supplemental to that of reference, and its metaphysics of presence.[41] Chains of vocal signs in the play of the sub-real are, for Senghor, rooted in a particular milieu, even as this logic might be seen to suggest something fundamental to language, suppressed in the Occidental theories of mimesis and signification from Plato to Saussure. What one finds in the emotional logic of *Négritude* is not intrinsic only to black expression, nor is it withheld from other cultural milieus but it is rather a logic that has thrived most extensively in the black African context and its diasporas, even as it has been repressed by the mimetic tradition of Europe. For Senghor, this logic of the signified as constitutive of the sign is located in the particularity of African culture and yet also proffered as a potential human universal—repressed in Western thought and aesthetics. It remains to be seen how Glissant, who certainly knew Senghor's work, nonetheless breaks with this logic of the universal and of universalism; relation, in brief, is not the universal but the passage of ideas across distinct cultural contexts.

As we see from this brief extract from Senghor's later writing, the tradition of Négritude is hardly merely the essentialism it has often been taken to be, but also offers an alternative theory of ontology and, most pertinently for present purposes, signification. This tradition of an alternative mode of signification, with which Glissant no doubt possesses a relation even as he departs from it, is combined in his work with an attention to the mixing of cultures that describes the Caribbean space from which he self-consciously writes. But, where Senghor's thought of the signified might be contrasted with Derrida's thought of the trace as an inverse but overlapping logic of signification and expression, Glissant's focus is not only on the logic of the sign but also on the cultural embeddedness— embeddedness in a "people," as we saw—of differing linguistic strategies: written and oral.

Rather than seeing oral and written cultures as markers on some teleological timeline, Glissant sees the condition of those colonized subjects strung between the two cultures as both a limitation to poetics and a potential opening point for a poetics of the future. For this future to arise, relation must be understood to be constitutive not only of apparent oral vernaculars and Creole intermixtures, but, indeed, of all languages. As Glissant puts it:

> If we speak of creolized cultures (like Caribbean cultures, for example) it is not to define a category that will by its very nature be opposed to other categories ('pure' cultures), but in order to assert that today infinite varieties of creolization are open to human conception, both on the level of awareness and on that of intention: in theory and in reality.[42]

Consequently: "[c]reolization as an idea means the negation of creolization as a category."[43] This theoretical assertion of the universal hybridity of language resonates strongly with Glissant's acknowledged poststructuralist interlocutors (Deleuze and Guattari's thought of the rhizome and the minor language, for instance) as well as with less acknowledged interlocutors—Derrida's notion of the "monolingualism of the other," for instance, which, as Celia Britton reminds us, was first presented as a paper at a conference organized by Glissant.[44] Yet, where Deleuze and Guattari's notion reaches radically and hurriedly toward the assertion and avowal of such universal Creolité in the sense they provide of a minor language, and where Derrida focuses on the constitutively alien aspect of language per se, even for the monolingualism of such a dominant language as French, Glissant is at pains to remark on the cross-cultural condition of alienation given in the denigration and isolation of so many Creoles. As such, however consonant Glissant is with a politics of global relation and relativization, he is also committed to a near-Fanonian exploration of the lived experience of the Creole speaker, with all her suffering of linguistic alienation and subjection.

In the essays on "Poetics" contained in *Caribbean Discourse*, Glissant orients the distinction between such colonizing languages as French and the Creoles that emerge to subvert and challenge them through a further distinction between "Natural" and "Forced" poetics. Reminiscent of Deleuze and Guattari's notion of a "minor literature," for Glissant, "Natural poetics" marks the condition whereby a tradition may linguistically challenge the structures of a language (whether the speaker is understood as insider of or outsider to the imagined community of said language) through "the most radical questioning of self-expression, extend, reform, clash with the given poetics."[45] Where "there is no incompatibility... between desire and expression," this natural poetics emerges at the margins of a dominant language to remake and reform it through the dominant language such that "[t]he most violent challenge to an established order can emerge from a natural poetics, when there is a continuity between the challenged order and the disorder that forces and negates it."[46] But Glissant is not willing to disavow the inherent limitations of the lived experience of the Creole, who, in being "haunted by the deep feeling of being different" finds the natural aspect of his poetics of resistance subject to a forced dimension.[47] Thus, he puts forward the idea that:

> [f]orced poetics exist where a need for expression confronts an inability to achieve expression [. . .] This is the case in the French Lesser Antilles, where the mother tongue, Creole, and the official language, French, produce in the Caribbean mind an unsuspected source of anguish.[48]

By relating constantly to the need to define itself and to assert itself against French, rather than ratify its own natural linguistic inclinations,

Creole is constantly forced to respond to the official language as a counterpoetics. As Glissant puts it, "forced poetics or counterpoetics is instituted by a community whose self-expression does not emerge spontaneously or result from an autonomous activity of the social body," rather Creole, a "primarily oral," and "not-yet-standardized" linguistic phenomenon finds its ability to harden itself into a standard field of signification from which natural poetics would emerge, thwarted by the degree to which its mode of expression has always been constituted by the attempt to eschew and escape the comprehension of the other.[49] Exemplifying this, Glissant annotates the way Creole oral expression takes on certain character precisely by its attempt to avoid comprehension by the colonizer. In Martinican Creole, he recounts, a certain frenetic rhythm is a requirement of spoken Creole, "not so much speed as a jumbled rush," such that what emerges is "the continuous stream of language that makes speech into one impenetrable block of sound," all so that the "*béké* masters" cannot understand or "manage this 'unstructured' use of language."[50] With this example of Creole's very rhythms emerging less (as Senghor would have it) from black African ontology, but (as Fanon would have it) from the lived experience of being in the gaze of the white *béké*, Glissant illustrates precisely the concrete instance of what he will develop more abstractly, that concept of closure that leads to a more effective openness: opacity. Creole is thwarted from producing a "natural poetics" by this condition of responsiveness and resistance to being understood by the colonizer, yet this cultivated opacity also proffers the prospect of a potentially novel poetics produced from the condition of opacity, or, what Glissant calls a "counterpoetics." In other words, if relation comes too readily in the face of differential conditions of power, it is not truly relation. Opacity, which can only be recognized as the deliberate, intentional relation to the other (or refusal thereof), proffers the possibility of a more robust and ethical relation in a future-to-come.

As such, while Glissant appears to have abandoned or withheld from Creole the utopianism of the minor linguistic power of the natural language, his realism about the lived experience of Creole therefore opens onto a further prospect of its acting as a productive and resistant linguistic strategy, into the future. Where "the poetically unsayable" emerges in the West, from the dignity of the human being that is tied to the status of being a property holding and owning subject, this self-sufficient Lockean personhood leads to a poetics of "transparency."[51] This transparency opens the subject and its subconscious to the individualism of expression associated with Western (and particularly Romantic) conceptions of genius. What it abandons for this individual expression, Glissant asserts, is the capacity to signify with and for the community. This "daring leap" of the human intentional subject, expressing itself as an individual

> allows us to argue that poetic passion, insofar as it requires a self, assumes, first, that the community has abandoned its basic right to be established and has been organized around the rights of the private individual. The poetically unsayable reflects the ultimate transformation of the economics of the right to private property. Paradoxically it is characterized by transparency and not opacity.[52]

Creole's opacity is deeply connected to the force of intention. The Creole idiom articulates itself in its opacity by a "deliberate ploy" on the part of the whole community to resist fixation, an intentional strategy that comes about through the communal consciousness of and resistance to the imprint of official, written language:

> In the historical circumstances that give rise to Creole, we can locate a forced poetics that is both an awareness of the restrictive presence of French as a linguistic background and the intentional attempt to reject French, that is, a conceptual system from which expression can be derived. Thus, imagery, that is, the "concrete" with all its metaphorical associations, is not, in the Creole language, an ordinary feature. It is a forced ploy (*détour forcé*).[53]

Hence, the concrete rhythms of Creole arise not from any ethnic, cultural, or even universal ontology, but as a concrete and deliberate, indeed intentional, strategy of relation: a negative relation of resistance to the dominance of the Other. Creole, then, reacts to French as counterpoetics, but this reaction is not a determination by French. Rather, in relating to this dominant Other, it produces an opacity of the entire community that opens onto but cannot wholly accomplish the prospect of a natural poetics. Yet Glissant's increasing exploration of relation might lead one to conjecture that Creole, in its negative opacity, is a relation to the other (rather than an ignorance of the world of the Occidental kind) that remains insufficient. It is a further relation that Glissant desires and promises. What Glissant desires instead, perhaps, is such an intentional strategy of relation that might risk openness over opacity, in a future-to-come where difference is recognized as the promise of relation across cultures and not as the transcendent determinism of the universal nor as the merely reactive (if strategically necessary) opacity of resistance—as a merely negative definition of a linguistic community. Opacity, as closure, ultimately, leads to a more robustly ethical openness, in a future relation.

One is tempted to venture into a series of the kind Glissant makes between the people and the author in light of his implicit historicization of the lived experience of the Creole-speaking subject. On the one hand, we have Occidental poetics, resembling very much the position of the author, whose access to the unsayable precedes as follows: Dignity—humanness—private property—individualism—the unsayable. On the other hand, Creole counterpoetics, in its opacity, is rendered through the following series: Indignity—dehumanization—chattel slavery—conscious opacity as resistance. Where the transparency of the poetics of the Western individual refuses the "(manifested) intention of a people" Glissant invokes as early as 1969's *Poetic Intention*, the poetics of opacity opens onto it, but according to a strange paradox. If opacity is the right of the community and the constantly escaping intention of the writer of Creole origin opens onto the expression of the whole Martinican Creole community, then, paradoxically, what is expressed is precisely the opacity of this communal expression. This imperative is doubled: what is desired is that the colonized writer express the whole community and infuse his written (often official "French" expression) with the trace of Creole orality. Yet in accomplishing this communal expression what emerges is not the epic of a people but the opaque impenetrability of this community as a totality—resistant to penetration and comprehension. Indeed, Glissant can be seen to manifest this strategy of writing the opaque community through the diegetic play present in his own novels. In the introduction to *Tout-monde*, he writes: "the book is constructed so that one cannot tell who is speaking... What is projected as speech encounters a multiple other who is the multiplicity of the world."[54]

So, if Creole represents a counterpoetics that remains forced, even as it is resistant in its opacity, what is the further step toward relation that Glissant desires? Rather than, *pace* Senghor, posit an alternative universality, Creole resists openness to the Other but in doing so maintains its specificity. The question becomes: at what moment does such a "minor" language, whose origins are a forced poetics, become a language that can maintain its opacity while moving into relation. Here, opacity becomes a kind of clearing out, a reach, a grasp, as with a clenched fist, which would relate to the Other on its own terms.

This is never universalism. Indeed, in *Caribbean Discourse*, Glissant explicitly refuses the desire to read Senghor as such a universalist, noting that "the part of M. Léopold Senghor's formulation most easily recognized in Western intellectual circles is that of the general idea of Universal Civilization."[55] One way to read Glissant's promise, then, is in the prospect that all languages, in embracing their opaque and historically specific hybridities, may consequently interact in a more concretely open poetics of relation. Yet before this is possible, the colonized must insist on their opacity, resisting a Western "generalizing universality" through the "stubborn insistence on *remaining where you are*."[56] If there is a relation to be had with the world as a whole, for Glissant, it cannot be an easy relation but must move painstakingly through this concrete insistence on situatedness. It is in this way that opacity can be read as a precondition of relation: a necessary (if insufficient) condition for poetic intention to open onto an alternative cross-cultural operation of relation: "poetic intention has always brought us to the absolute prescience of the Whole-world."

For Glissant, the ghostly presence of the intention of the author, circuitously open to a communal opacity and such an opacity will have always marked the path to relation, openness, and the worldwide embrace of difference. Yet this conception translates gradually into an increasing optimism on the poet's part across his career, as Britton has noted.[57] As Alexandre Leupin has observed, this can be read as a correction (rather than a contradiction) of Hegel's notion of history.[58] Glissant shows the difference insisted upon by the poststructuralists to be enriched by a project of overcoming in the face of the historical condition of the colonized (just as Hegelian ontology was, for Fanon, a project initially thwarted by the "lived experience" of racism). As Fanon puts it, "There is in fact a 'being for 'other,' as described by Hegel, but any ontology is made impossible in a colonized and acculturated society."[59] If 2006's *In Praise of Difference and of the Different* explicitly connects intention to relation, as we have seen, it begins and ends with that most Hegelian of aesthetic anchor points, beauty, which for Glissant is equally aligned with freedom as it is for Hegel.[60]

While both Hegel and Glissant see aesthetic beauty as directed toward the future, the difference for the latter—from as late as 1969—arises less from a predetermined culmination of self-conscious freedom's historical telos than in the spontaneous emergence of cross-cultural interlocution through willful relation. If then, the infusion of Creole orality inscribes itself through a willful opacity within Caribbean writing (and, indeed, postcolonial literature more generally), then it is the first step toward a circularity and openness which would proffer the prospect of an equal acknowledgment of difference: intention leading to an embrace of difference at the level of the "whole-world." Thus, the later Glissant will assert that "[e]very poetic intention leads straight to a narrative of the whole world, for which this narrative is not a narrative but a state of relatedness of the state of differences within a delimited space, confined or expanding, it depends, and in a given period of time."[61] Yet, one notices here that narrative is doubled and challenged even as it is avowed. To arrive at the culmination point of a relatedness that will lead Glissant to avow this non-narrative "state of relatedness" the younger Glissant will have to have sublated Hegel.

This is so, in *Poetic Intention*, not only when Hegel is explicitly named as an interlocutor: "himself a prisoner of the parenthesis [...] in which he encloses Africa."[62] It is also the case whenever Glissant names and develops his own concept of the relation of the colonized to a capitalized "History"—a trope that marks not the narration of the passing of time for imagined communities per se, but the colonizing total history of the Occident of which Hegel marks the sign *par excellence*. The relation of histories unsettles this capitalized "History," rendering it impossible; thus: "[w]here histories meet, History comes to an end."[63] In *Poetic Intention*, Glissant's notion of relatedness in historical time hinges on a new conception of what he calls "duration," which is to be reconstituted as non-linear and relative—presaging what he will later call "circular" as opposed to "arrow-like nomadism."[64] Duration, with its attention to temporality, is, one could argue, not unlike (though not identical with) Senghor's conception of rhythmic ontology. As he continues in the earlier essays: "If we deny duration: then at last we will have conquered, full and durable, the fantastic burgeoning of the instant, for all, in the joyful concern for all."[65] While Glissant acknowledges the role of "duration," as a certain trajectory of reckoning the unity (and teleology) of "History," in the avowal of worldwide relation ("the house of the We"), the beginning of relation is, he argues, the willful disavowal of the duration of History in order to give way to an uncertain but open meeting of cultures. As he puts it, "[y]es, what duration carries into the instant is the sacrament (the vow) of commonality."[66] Glissant then acknowledges the role of Universal history in Universal humanism and commonality;

what he objects to and adds, supplementing this unitary "commonality," is an alternate vow, the "vow of the Other," which calls for an ongoing relatedness. If Senghor was a kind of inverse Hegelian, proffering an alternate account of the Universal from the perspective of African ontology, Glissant maneuvers between the Scylla of Hegelian Universal History and the Charybdis of Négritude toward a Caribbean perspective of difference and cross-cultural interaction. Glissant's poetics of relation, then, begins with the denial of "History" as a determinative force: "If we deny duration: we will have left the iniquity of *one* History, in order to enter into the nation, poetics, histories—commuted, labyrinthine, vital."[67] It is this turn from the unitary History of the universal (whether of Hegel or of Senghor) that leads Glissant to the assertion uniting our twin concerns: "[i]ntention thus perfects itself in Relation."[68]

In so connecting conscious intention as a rejection of monolithic "History" to the beginning of a relation between histories, Glissant will perform a retooling of logic of the signified we found in Senghor, retooled and redeployed not to proffer an antithesis to history via African ontology, but instead to avow a mobile model for a rooted intentionality that moves from the particular to the different (rather than the universal). As he puts it, several pages on, "the vow of poetry [...] will have to conquer its simplicity right up against the split injunction where knowledge has led man: to be consciousness and denied science of consciousness."[69] By avowing the intentional eschewal of double-consciousness through poetic invention, the poet is able to return full plenitude to signification rather than rest on mimetic and representational modes alone, the risk which Glissant identifies as the moment when "sign and signifier [are merely] falling from the signified."[70] For Glissant

> The poet chooses, elects in the mass of the world what he must preserve, what his song is attuned to. And *rhythm* is ritual force, lever of consciousness . . . It names the Drama that is ours: fire of the Diverse, struggle of the Disparate, vow of the Other. In chaos, it perpetuates this work, which is that of poetry alone: to fell walls, bark; to unify without denaturing, order without taxidermizing, unveil without destroying; to know at last each thing and this space between one thing and another, these saps, these countries—at the sharpest of the spirit and the magnanimity of the heart.[71]

For Glissant, then, Senghorian rhythm will remain as a conscious choice in the path from opacity to that of relation.

Where Derrida emphasizes the slippage of all signification and Senghor the role of the signified's sonic rhythm, Glissant asserts that an openness to an (inevitably forestalled) poetic intention replaces History with relation and in so doing might restore, if only in momentary and fleeting encounters, the full plenitude of the sign. Avoiding any metaphysics of presence, Glissant's thought of opacity through the willful command of duration asserts that, in recognizing the role of relation, minority, trace, and difference, apparent in Creole as fundamental to all languages (however much they might represent themselves as whole and unitary), one comes to a fuller recognition of the presence that was always trace. So far so good; yet one might ask how this differs from the Deleuzian-Guattarian or Derridean conceptions of language I have already catalogued? It does so through Glissant's recognition of the concrete experience of history given to the subject of Creole in relation to the official language of the colonizer. Where the poststructuralists (Deleuze and Guattari in particular) embrace a rhizomatic logic of intersecting minor languages with no dominant formations as settled in advance, Glissant insists on a Fanonian passage through the historical and lived experience of the speaker of the minor language, which is no less historical in its disavowal of "History." The self-conscious opacity of the poetic intention of the colonized functions as a "vow of the Other," which guarantees a "whole-world" given not in the claim of the Universal but in a steadfast alterity that better promises a futurity of relation, of difference and the different—in a newly opened play of the world-historical.[72] A network—a relation—of opaque and unique particulars offers a distributed immanence, greater than any claim of universality and what emerges is the negation of ethnocentrism and the embrace of the whole-world.

Notes

1. Édouard Glissant, *Poetic Intention*. Trans Nathanaël. New York: Nightboat, 2010, 201.
2. Roland Barthes, "The Death of the Author," in *Image, Music, Text*, trans. Stephen Heath. New York: Hill and Wang, 1988, 142–148; Michel Foucault, "What is an Author?" in *The Foucault Reader*, ed. Paul Rabinow, New York: Pantheon, 1984, 101–120; Jacques Derrida, "Différance," in *Margins of Philosophy*, trans. Alan Bass. Chicago: University of Chicago Press, 1982, 1–28.

3. Michael Wiedorn, "Glissant's 'Philosophie De La Relation': 'I Have Spoken the Chaos of Writing in the Ardor of the Poem,'" in *Callaloo* 36, 4 (2013): 902–915, 908–909.
4. See Tim Watson, *Culture Writing: Literature and Anthropology in the Midcentury Atlantic World*. Oxford: Oxford University Press, 2018.
5. Édouard Glissant, "In Praise of the Different and of Difference," trans. Celia Britton, *Callaloo* 34, 4 (2013): 856–862, 860.
6. The overlap identified by Celia Britton, between Glissant and, on the one hand, Barthes, Foucault, and Derrida as well as, on the other, their Anglo-American postcolonial inheritors (principally Homi Bhabha and Gayatri Chakravorty Spivak), should lead us, as Britton further suggests, to see the field of anti-colonial literary criticism as fundamentally given to a process of relation that has fluidly traversed the Atlantic. See Britton, *Edouard Glissant and Postcolonial Theory: Strategies of Language and Resistance*. Charlottesville: University of Virginia Press, 1999.
7. Glissant, *Poetics of Relation*, trans. Betsy Wing, Ann Arbor: University of Michigan Press, 1997, 111–120, 189–194.
8. Glissant, *Poetics of Relation*, 6.
9. Glissant, *Poetics of Relation*, 7.
10. John E. Drabinski, *Glissant and the Middle Passage: Philosophy, Beginning, Abyss*. Minneapolis: University of Minnesota Press, 2019, 16.
11. This concept is elaborated by Derrida initially in *Of Grammatology*, trans. Gayatri Chakravorty Spivak, Baltimore: Johns Hopkins University Press, 1976. Its development across his oeuvre is too frequent to annotate here.
12. I employ Paul Gilroy's phrase since it most succinctly and richly describes the reality of the past, present, and indeed future of the globalizing communities that are, I think, closest to Glissant's own paradigm. Gilroy, *The Black Atlantic: Modernity and Double Consciousness*. London: Verso, 1993.
13. Glissant, *Poetics of Relation*, 23.
14. Glissant *Poetic Intention*, 30.
15. Glissant, *Poetics of Relation*, 11.
16. Glissant, *Poetics of Relation*, 26.
17. Jacques Rancière, *Disagreement: Politics and Philosophy*. Minneapolis: University of Minnesota Press, 2004.

18. Glissant, *Caribbean Discourse: Selected Essays*, ed. and trans. J. Michael Dash. Charlottesville: University Press of Virginia, 1989, 88. All references to this text are paginated to this English edition. Many of my citations have been altered slightly from the text of this English edition, in consultation with *Le Discourse Antillais*. Paris: Éditions Du Seuil, 1981. Where alterations have been made, they are marked "translation modified."
19. "Soleil de la Conscience" both appeared in 1956 published autonomously and was republished in 1969's more extended collection of writings, *Poetic Intention*.
20. Barthes, "Death of the Author," 143.
21. Barthes, "Death of the Author," 143.
22. Barthes, "Death of the Author," 143.
23. Glissant, *The Fourth Century*, trans. Betsy Wing. Lincoln: University of Nebraska Press, 2001, 180.
24. Glissant, *The Fourth Century*, 180.
25. Wiedorn, "Glissant's 'Philosophie De La Relation,'" 910.
26. Glissant, *The Fourth Century*, 167.
27. Barthes, "Death of the Author," 143.
28. Glissant, *Caribbean* Discourse, 137.
29. John Locke, *Two Treatises of Government*, ed. Peter Laslett, Cambridge: Cambridge University Press, 2003.
30. Fanon, *Black Skin White Masks*, xi.
31. Yet, Glissant also affords attention to his own situation as a postcolonial writer, as well as his annotation of New World writers from Saint-John Perse to Faulkner and to Fanon (indeed to his own work), with their own complex relation to the Occidental world and its canon, as well, indeed, as emphasizing the precarious place of the oral and Creole (an emphasis the ironically more Western-centric Said eschews).
32. Glissant, *Poetic Intention*, 30. Translation modified.
33. Glissant, *Poetic Intention*, Translation modified.
34. Édouard Glissant and Alexandre Leupin, *The Baton Rouge Interviews*, trans. Kate M. Cooper. Liverpool: Liverpool University Press, 2020, 32.
35. Glissant *Poetic Intention*, 201.
36. Derrida, "Signature, Event, Context," 326.
37. Derrida, "Signature, Event, Context," 326.

38. Souleymane Bachir Diagne, *African Art as Philosophy: Senghor, Bergson, and the Idea of Negritude*, trans. Chike Jeffers, London: Seagull, 2011; see especially 45–96.
39. Léopold Sédar Senghor, "De La Négritude," in *Liberté V: Le Dialogue Des Cultures*. Paris: Editions du Seuil, 1993, 22. Author's translation.
40. Senghor, "Ce Que L'Homme Noir Apporte," in *Liberté I: Négritude et Humanisme*. Paris: Editions du Seuil, 1964, 22–38. Translation available as "What the Black Man Contributes," trans. Mary Beth Mader in *Race and Racism in Continental Philosophy*, ed. Robert Bernasconi and Sybol Cook, Bloomington: Indiana University Press, 2003, 287–302.
41. Indeed, the later Derrida at one point declared: "so long ago I substituted the concept of trace for that of signifier." See Derrida, "And Say the Animal Responded?" trans. David Wills in *Zoontologies: The Question of the Animal*, ed. Cary Wolfe, Minneapolis: University of Minnesota Press, 2003, 137.
42. Glissant, *Caribbean Discourse*, 140.
43. Glissant, *Caribbean Discourse*, 141.
44. On Deleuze and Guattari's concept of minor literature, see their *Kafka: Toward a Minor Literature*, trans. Dana Polan, Minneapolis: University of Minnesota Press, 1986. On Derrida's concept, see his *Monolingualism of the Other, or the Prosthesis of Origin*, trans. Patrick Mensah, Stanford: Stanford University Press, 1998. Britton remarks on the occasion of Derrida's lecture in *Édouard Glissant and Postcolonial Theory*, 5.
45. Glissant, *Caribbean Discourse*, 120.
46. Glissant, *Caribbean Discourse*, 120.
47. Glissant, *Caribbean Discourse*, 121.
48. Glissant, *Caribbean Discourse*, 120.
49. Glissant, *Caribbean Discourse*, 121.
50. Glissant, *Caribbean Discourse*, 124.
51. Glissant, *Caribbean Discourse*, 137.
52. Glissant, *Caribbean Discourse*, 137. In keeping with Glissant's French text, I have modified the translation to substitute "opacity" for Dash's close but, in English, somewhat misleading "obscurity." Glissant uses the word *obscurité*.
53. Glissant, *Caribbean Discourse*, 126. Translation modified.

54. Glissant, *Tout-Monde*. Paris: Gallimard, 1993, 131. Author's translation.
55. Glissant, *Caribbean Discourse*, 139.
56. Glissant, *Caribbean Discourse*, 139.
57. Britton, *Édouard Glissant and Postcolonial Theory*, 11–34.
58. Alexandre Leupin, "The Slave's Jouissance," in *Callaloo* 36, 4 (2013): 891–901.
59. Frantz Fanon, *Black Skin, White Masks*, trans. Richard Philcox, New York: Grove Press, 2008, 89.
60. Yet where, for Hegel, aesthetic beauty expressed freedom through the teleological path toward the perfection of spirit's realization in self-consciousness, for Glissant, beauty is "nascent beauty," the site wherein "old differences are outlined and future differences stir." Glissant, "In Praise of Difference and the Different," 862.
61. Glissant, "In Praise of Difference and the Different." 860.
62. Glissant, *Poetic Intention*, 31.
63. Glissant, *Poetic Intention*, 199.
64. Glissant, *Poetics of Relation*, 11–14.
65. Glissant, *Poetic Intention*, 201.
66. Glissant, *Poetic Intention*, 201.
67. Glissant, *Poetic Intention*, 201.
68. Glissant, *Poetic Intention*, 201.
69. Glissant, *Poetic Intention*, 207.
70. Glissant, *Poetic Intention*, 207.
71. Glissant, *Poetic Intention*, 206–207. Emphasis Added.
72. Gayatri Chakravorty Spivak, *The Postcolonial Critic: Interviews, Strategies, Dialogues*, ed. Sarah Harasym, London: Routledge, 1990, 15.

CHAPTER 4

An Appetite to Begin: Intention and the Political in the Work of Edward Said

Abstract This chapter mines both the published work of Edward Said and his archived correspondence to articulate his shifting and developing attitude to a number of paradigms of literary analysis: notably poststructuralist thought and, also, the idea of authorial intention. Said can be seen to have responded to Barthes in 1973's book *Beginnings: Intention and Method* wherein he made the case for a way of thinking about the "appetite to begin" as an important way of reconceiving intentionalism anew. The chapter draws on key lines of thought at crucial junctures in Said's career, from the essays of *The World, The Text, and the Critic*—where, among much else, Said drew on medieval Islamic scholarship and its various attitudes to text and interpretation—the masterful work of *Orientalism*, the construction of *Beginnings*, and it tracks attempts to problematize and critique poststructuralism in later works such as *Culture and Imperialism*.

Keywords Edward Said · Authorship · Decolonization · Michel Foucault · Poststructuralism · Intention in literature

In the wake of Barthes' staggering intervention, as Glissant was rewriting the emerging tenets of poststructuralism on the question of authorship, where was Edward Said? Did he miss the debates on structure, discourse, and authorship of the 1960s and beyond? An obvious answer is: of course not! Said was exposed to structuralist thought and poststructuralist theory from as early as 1966 when he attended the landmark conference on "The Languages of Criticism and the Science of Man" at the invitation of J. Hillis Miller.[1] Said began reading and working, in earnest, on the structuralist and poststructuralist thinkers, particularly Michel Foucault and a number of essays appeared both in the lead-up to his 1975 book *Beginnings: Intention and Method* (some forming a part of it) and in its wake. Nonetheless, despite some correspondence, in the early 1970s, Said and Foucault were ships in the night; Said and Roland Barthes, too. He had sent each of these writers articles of his that referred to and explored their work. On the 25 of August, 1972, Barthes sent off a reply, extolling the virtues of Said's work—"so fair, so subtle, so well observed"—and suggested they meet should the latter make it to Paris.[2] Foucault, on receiving a 1972 article by Said for *boundary 2* replied in a handwritten note with just as much enthusiasm.[3] "I infinitely admire," Foucault wrote, "your intelligence, your mastery, and the rigor of your analysis to the point that you have helped me to clarify the nature of my own future work. I greatly hope that we will have occasion to meet."[4] Despite this ebullient praise and overtures of meeting, neither Barthes nor Foucault met Said when he did indeed pass through Paris in March and April of 1973 after a year spent on a Guggenheim Fellowship in Beirut. Barthes sent an apology that he would be in Italy for these months.[5] Said would not meet Foucault till the end of the decade by which time, his intellectual relationship with poststructuralism had soured, even as his impression of the *maître à penser* Foucault showed some sign of its having been tainted.[6]

Of course there is more than a modicum of allusion in my discussing Said and his French interlocutors as missing each other ever so slightly. While I do not mean it to be entirely allegorical I am neither only interested in the literal events: the literal fact of Said and Foucault "meeting" or not, or on what date and at which place. Nonetheless, when I speak of Said "missing" Barthes and Foucault, I do not mean to suggest crudely that Said did not understand them. But this literal experience of not quite crossing physical paths with the French poststructuralists, I think, reflects an emergent logic in his work. While Said initially embraced the novel avant-garde philosophical and critical elaborations of language represented by such French thinkers, as his biographer Timothy Brennan stresses, by the nineteen-eighties he would come to see the postmodernism that then dominated in Anglo-American literary studies and, to some degree, the poststructuralism he had earlier embraced as unrewarding, possibly even aligned with political repression. He would even compare theory's effects to Ronald Reagan's politics in the contemporary United States.[7] According to Brennan, "Said often referred to 'theory' as 'the new New Criticism,' implying that the staid literary formalism of the 1950s had simply changed clothes in the 1980s, appearing now in the insurrectionary costume of deconstruction, Lacanian psychoanalysis, and postmodernism."[8] Between the enthusiasm of the 1970s and the turn in the 1980s toward humanism and the manifest presence of the public intellectual, clearly something shifted in Said's view of poststructuralism and postmodernism. And, indeed, the latter dismissals are quite well known. I want to suggest that this was not a case of Said's having naively missed something in the thought of Foucault or Derrida, but rather it was a case of a sense of dissatisfaction earlier on, being confirmed and amplified as time wore on. In this chapter I explore this sense of difference between Said's intellectual emphases and those of the French theorists and suggest that his difference with them always lay in his strong emphasis on agency in the work of social change, despite his recognition of the useful dimensions of such ideas as were given in discursive analysis. Indeed it may be the case that what Said restores of humanism to discursive method is what had been missed by key poststructuralists and their followers.[9]

Said's later statements about poststructuralism and its apolitical dimension are, then, well known. What has been less well explored, however, is the complexity of Said's earliest engagement with structuralism and poststructuralism as he seemingly paradoxically moved to emphasize an intentionalist position in literary interpretation. Said's work in the early 1970s, then, signals an emergent critique of poststructuralism's rejection of authorial imprint, critical reception, and the role of the context that circulates around texts, implying their agency and meaning in the world. Before I begin to outline this analysis of Said's early texts, it would do to return briefly to Said and Foucault's actual meeting—though disappointingly for all concerned, this turns out to be for the most part a non-encounter. Their actual meeting would take place in 1979, when Foucault's house was used as the location for a summit on Middle East peace held by an aging Jean Paul Sartre and his journal *Les Temps Modernes*. Said describes Foucault as showing little or no interest in the peace talks, leaving everyday at his usual time to visit the archives.[10]

This must have been a double disappointment to Said since it was not only intellectual admiration that had led him to Foucault nearly a decade earlier. Foucault had, in 1972 signed an open letter in *Le Monde* initiated by Philippe Sollers, which made a call for the Palestinian people (*appel pour les Palestinians*)—a response to the 1972 war which continued the violent process of occupation and displacement to which the Palestinian people had been subjected.[11] Foucault had not yet come to take on the, at turns, apathetic and, even, Zionist positions, he would later turn to.[12] Therefore, Foucault's signature on Sollers's note of solidarity and with it his embrace of these marginalized and colonized people—Said's people—inspired a profound response in the latter. Responding a few months after Foucault's note had been sent to him from Beirut, Said noted that Jean Genet (who had visited him there) had told Said that Foucault, along with Deleuze, Sollers, and Derrida, "are pro-Palestinian."[13] Since, he wrote to Foucault, he "had seen 'l'appel pour les Palestiniens' which you have signed. So to my intellectual admiration, I add my Palestinian gratitude. And politically — I am Palestinian."[14] He wrote further that he had "sensed" in Foucault's "theoretical work" such "revolutionary trajectories."[15] The degree to which this sense was misplaced would be consequential both as a moment of political differentiation and as a site for Said to explore within his own thought.

Said also knew Barthes' work well enough to know that his own idea of beginning intention lay in opposition to the notion of the death of the author that had been aired only a few years earlier. Midway through *Beginnings* he would say as much, in a manner both assertive and delicate:

> For despite recent genuinely investigative tendencies in criticism (in, for example, the work of Roland Barthes), certain conventions, persisting as unexamined vestiges of the whole history of ideas, have a strong hold upon the critical imagination as it tries to grasp what a text exactly is. Such a determination is of quite basic importance. Thus certain questions—such as the nature of the author's (beginning and continued) authority over his text, the beginnings and development of an author's work, the location in time and society of a text, and the possibility of the sequential construction of a literary totality viewed as an ensemble of made relationships—remain relevant.[16]

The justification for this polite disagreement would be elaborated throughout the book. It would not be until 1978 that Said offered his most full engagement with Jacques Derrida's thought—in an article on

Derrida and Foucault for *Critical Inquiry*. He would recognize Derrida's brilliance even as he found it overly vested in the textual, ungiven to politics—a charge that has indeed been made and refuted by numerous others over the years. Whether one thinks, along with Said that deconstruction is vested in text (with "nothing outside," etc.) or whether one takes seriously the broader deconstructive emphasis on trace and iterability, which takes literal text merely as a paradigm case for the broader metaphysics of presence is difficult to resolve in this chapter alone. Pertinent to an account of Said's thought about authorship and its effects though is the basis for Said's preference for Foucault over Derrida. Whether one finds in Derrida a degree of relation between text and power (for instance in the deconstruction of logocentrism), there is no doubt that Foucault's thought at this time—particularly in the *Archeology of Knowledge*—was methodologically engaged with the relation between such textual and archival analysis and with the world of institutions. This is evident enough in a moment of culmination in Said's 1978 essay:

> I will not go so far as to say that Derrida's own position amounts to a new orthodoxy. But I can say that it has not, from its unique vantage point, illuminated in sufficient detail the thing he refers to in his account of *le corps enseignant* [bodies of knowledge], that is, *le contrat entre ces corps* [the contract between these bodies] (bodies of knowledge, institutions, power), a contract hidden because *jamais exhibe sur le devant de la scene* [never exhibited on the stage]. All of Derrida's work has magnificently demonstrated that such a contract exists, that texts demonstrating logocentric biases are indications that the contract exists and keeps existing from period to period in Western history and culture. But it is a legitimate question, I think, to ask what keeps that contract together, what makes it possible for a certain system of metaphysical ideas, as well as a whole structure of concepts, praxes, ideologies derived from it, to maintain itself from Greek antiquity up through the present. What forces keep all these ideas glued together? What forces get them into texts?[17]

Said, then, both mastered a reading of French thinkers such as Barthes, Foucault, and Derrida even as he would strategically break with each of them to varying degrees, specifically in the lead-up to his book *Beginnings* and its immediate aftermath, though also as he developed his political history of orientalism in the book of that name and indeed, within his book on "method"—the collection of essays called *The World, The Text and the Critic*.[18] Where he did break with these poststructuralisms was, I suggest around two central issues: first the status of the authorial imprint on a text—its agency and presence (what he called "beginning intention") and second around the question of power, not only how it circulates and manifests through structures but how it is implemented and wielded—and intentionally so. In this manner, Said's literary and political analysis come together: power begins, at any moment, to make the world.

Two Visions in (and Around) *Beginnings*

In March of 1973, Edward Said wrote to his publisher Edwin Glikes, expressing some qualified doubts about the book manuscript he was pulling together at that time: "As I look back over what I've just written I see that it is pretty sketchy, but I'm so deeply in the book now that it's hard to get out and say short things about it."[19] In June he would feel somewhat more confident, writing to his dissertation advisor, Harvard Professor Monroe Engel, with a mix of emotions on nearing completion of his book; the book was *Beginnings*. There he reveals that he had rethought the project of the essays he had been writing on the related topics of beginnings (as opposed to origins), intention, method, idiosyncrasy, and orientation to the readerly community. Said was beginning to imagine the essays with more of the coherence and continuity of a book: "You remember those essays that Basic [books] is to publish. Well I rewrote them all, and now I have no essays at all, but a book (all but the last chapter) of some value I think."[20] He went on to develop his sense of why he intuitively felt its value:

> At least it's been exhilarating —and hard—because I felt the freedom of virtually creating the subject as I went along (the subject, perhaps you remember is beginning). Thus I discussed what I wanted to, no prescribed material, no ritualistic attempts to 'cover' scholarly studies, etc.[21]

He would then proceed to outline the book before continuing with his sense of its potential value: "It's full of theory but not, I think, anything bloodless. But all year I've been obsessed with how unscholarly I am, so I put in half my time trying to remedy the holes."[22] What are these holes? What tensions creep into the structure of *Beginnings* or, indeed, infiltrate its argument? Was Said worried about living up to the work of these French thinkers, or (and as I suggest more likely), was he worried about their rejection of authorship and embrace of discourse (to name two key concepts) conflicting with his own strong methodological and political convictions about agency and power? My contention, which I hope is unfolding, is that while he deeply grasped the efficacy of poststructural analysis to show the distributed capillary movement of power, he increasingly found himself troubled over the totalizing postulate of such structure without any agency, textuality without even any trace of an author.

In an interview published in *diacritics* in 1976, shortly after the publication of *Beginnings*, Said makes two clear statements about authorship which would at first blush appear in contradistinction. "Nothing," he says, "in a text merely occurs or happens; a text is made—by the author, the critic, the reader—and it is a collective enterprise to a certain extent."[23] Yet later, in the same interview, Said will suggest, limning Foucault, something that sounds antithetical: "[w]riting is not free, nor is it performed uniquely by a sovereign writer who writes more or less as he or she pleases. Writing belongs to a system of utterances that has all sorts of affiliative, often constricting relationships with the world of nations, as Vico called it."[24] In this way, Said avows the *making* of texts, their relation with their readers and those authors that produce them. But he also fully grasps the lesson of the utterance and of discourse as each ensnares any authorial intent. Said was at this time (and arguably remained still, to some degree) steeped in Foucault's ideas of discourse and of the play of statements (in other words, archeology): an elaboration of the way categories operate at a particular epistemic moment and their relation to power and time (to name two of such a method's correlatives only). While not an example of some manner of reductive or limiting contradiction, it is instead, I suggest, an attempt to combine together two ostensibly divergent convictions: the one that texts are made (most especially by the authors who begin them) and the other—more Foucauldian—conviction that "[w]riting belongs to a system of utterances." Said was both aware of the risk of contradiction and determined to resolve these apparent paradoxes into productive revelations. Indeed, where Said believed in syncretism, he did not believe in the neat synthesis associated with Hegelian thinking. As Brennan records, "[i]n the early 1970s, he explained the rationale for his seminar reading list to students as being made up of writers who are, 'anti-dialectical in the sense that dialectics as Hegel used it provided for a final transcendence and/or resolution.'"[25] If Said's own sense of syncretic thinking resembles his teaching at the period, then it is anti-dialectical in this sense. Perhaps, then, the sense of discourse and of writerly agency was one he believed productive in itself and more so where it is not finally resolved or transcended.

Said writes of his own project in his 1975 book that beginnings are given to an intention, a "choice," one capable of "making and producing difference," it connects to "authority" and is distinct from an origin.[26] On this last point as in so many things, Said is drawing explicitly on seventeenth- and eighteenth-century Italian philosopher Giambattista Vico. For Said, an origin is causal but not willed, it is akin to a divine or natural order of filiation. As Said writes, "ideas about origins, because of their passivity, are put to uses I believe ought to be avoided."[27] Or, quite simply: "beginning and beginning again are historical, whereas origins are divine."[28] Like Glissant, Said rejects the utility of searches after origins, in favor of a beginning, whose structural place in the former is not unlike the mobile alluvium of the sea floor discussed in Chapter 2.

Writing of nineteenth-century French orientalist Ernst Renan's *Life of Jesus* and of the traditional of the Gospels more generally, Said observes that:

> The text leaves behind its origin (which in the case of the New Testament is Jesus) for the text is the beginning of a series of substitutions which altogether comprise the formal object we call a text. This is neither as tautological nor as metaphysical as it seems. Every text is something first composed, then transmitted, then received, then edited and interpreted, then reconsidered. Yet the moment that composition-the setting of pen to paper-takes place, each of these processes is somehow involved: since there is really no such thing as an absolutely primal text, each act of composition involves other texts, and so each writing transmits itself, receives other writing, is an interpretation of other writing, reconstitutes (by displacement) other writing.[29]

Said here elegantly differentiates between origin and beginning. Just as Vico suggested that what he called "gentile" writing broke with the divinely ordained logic of the word in, say, the Hebrew Bible, Said also sees willful acts of composition and dissemination as his focus: beginnings and not origins.[30] As Said says late in the text, "beginnings are eminently secular, or gentile, continuing activities." Indeed, as Said develops the distinction, a beginning intends meaning but the continuities and methods developing from it are generally *orders* of *dispersion,* of *adjacency,* and of *complementarity.* A different way of putting this is to say that whereas an origin *centrally* dominates what derives from it, the beginning (especially the modern beginning), encourages nonlinear development, a logic given to the sort of multileveled coherence of dispersion we find in Freud's text, in the texts of modern writers, or in Foucault's archeological investigations.[31]

He emphasizes the modes of acting, meaning, and intending that go into any process of writing such as to both avow and not fetishize the pre-inscriptive act of writing.

Glissant and Said, then, each differentiate a contingent beginning from an early, powerful, and notably lost sense of origin. Where Said's notion of a beginning differs from the mobile alluvium of Glissant is in the historically specific location of beginnings that the latter finds in the contradictions of the middle passage. The consequences are such that where Said emphasizes the willed capacity of the beginning, Glissant emphasizes the chaos that the alluvial unleashes on memory and the profound sense of loss associated with the subject of Caribbean and wider dispossession.

This is not to say that Said ignores dispossession. His own double dispossession from Jerusalem to Cairo to the United States would of course have consequences for his thinking. In the essay "Reflections on Exile," for instance, Said begins his essay by suggesting that exile is a compelling ground of thought even as it is a horror to live through: "Exile is strangely compelling to think about but terrible to experience. It is the unhealable rift forced between a human being and a native place, between the self and its true home: its essential sadness can never be surmounted."[32] We might hear echoes in this "unhealable rift" of exile in Glissant's notion of "the panic of the new land," coupled with "the haunting of the old land."[33] Similarly Said also sees those echoes of memory we have found in Glissant's reflection on the rift: "For an exile, habits of life, expression, or activity in the new environment inevitably occur against the memory of these things in another environment."[34] While the notion of beginning in Said and the trope of the alluvial in Glissant are not identical, each of them responds to the sense of imagination and loss given in differing but comparable experiences of exile.

Said sees the whole writing process as just as differentiated and deferred as any poststructuralist does however, he implicitly insists that the critic hold onto a sense of the act of willful intention involved in not only composition but revision and editing. Following Vico, Said is invested in

> [t]he so-called metaphysical point [that] then becomes conation—what in this book I have been calling beginning intention—which in history is human will, understood both temporally and absolutely. Human will, we recall, is the property of humanity, and as such it is radically less effective than divine will; but it is nonetheless an imperfect model of divine will, albeit an imperfect one.[35]

This last claim comes not from the beginning of Said's book but from its end: the concluding chapter on Vico. This is because one argument of the present chapter is that much of Said's intentions for *Beginnings*—his passionate commitment to the act of writing—developed and were unleashed only for the 1975 book. Said's sense of beginnings develops through the early chapters and indeed, the conclusion (perhaps there most of all). If we consider that Chapter 4, which departs from a reading of Jean Piaget to consider the position and meaning of what we typically call a *text* was previously published in *Modern Language Notes* in 1970. And if we also note that the fourth chapter, which treats Barthes, Foucault, and Derrida—"*Abecadarium Culturae:* Absence, Writing, Statement, Discourse, Archeology, Structuralism"—was published in *Triquarterly* in 1971, we can surmise something about the argument of the book as a whole. Chapter 4 sustained emphasis on structure and discourse, because it was disseminated (and likely composed) earlier than the book's 1973 assemblage, necessitated a certain reconciliation with Said's ideas about the *making* of texts and the beginning intention this idea implies.

To my knowledge, the earlier chapters and, without doubt, the conclusion were largely written in 1973 during the sabbatical year Said spent in Beirut and revised up to the book's publication. In this light, we have an explanation for the more extensive examination of and emphasis on beginning intention in the introduction and earlier chapters (and the conclusion on Vico) rather than the two articles that became chapter four and five. In writing *Beginnings*, Said wrestled with the statement and explored the meaning of the discursive but ultimately the position it takes is, through his framing, one strongly emphasizing making.

Thus in so far as he wrote whole chapters on Foucault and his compatriot theorists, Said was enamored of their bold experiment with language, discourse, and structure. But in so far as it butted up against his intentionalist convictions: that texts are made and relate to the world, Said needed some way to generatively approach poststructuralist thought while not consigning the beginning intention to the dustbin of discourse. For this reason, Said insisted within the pages of *Beginnings* that a beginning intention was not the same thing as an author. For example, in discussing Freud and Nietzsche, he would note that,

> an intention in the psychoanalytic discourse is the immediate practical application of the mutuality between men which ensues when a repressive central authority is removed. Nietzsche's distinctions between *origin* and *purpose* in the passage that follows correspond to the distinctions I have been making between *author* (origin) and *beginning intention* (purpose and interpretation).[36]

The kind of imprint that Said was exploring was not reducible to the knowing subject traditionally called the author and for that reason, he, in a sense, accepted the notion of the author subject's "death." While each logic is intentionalist, the beginning emerges from his book as developed with greater nuance. He writes, early in *Beginnings*:

> we do not possess a manageable existential category for writing—whether that of an "author," a "mind," or a "Zeitgeist"—strong enough on the basis of what happened or existed before the present writing to explain what is happening in the present writing or where it begins.[37]

Authorship is, then, perhaps too extensive a concept and yet simultaneously, not "strong enough" to explain the beginning of writing. For Said, beginning is a form of activity that can be described and one that remains distinct from seeing in authorship and authority a fixed and immutable point of subjectivity and being. Beginning is a process or, as Said prefers, an appetite; it is not a fixed identity or even subjectivity. Nonetheless, from the very beginning, Said presents beginnings as willful, if revisable, acts: "[b]eginning is not only a kind of action; it is also a frame of mind, a kind of work, an attitude, a consciousness."[38] Yet such a concept as text, which would be defined implicitly in poststructuralist works as given to the trappings of structure, sign, and play (to use one such formulation), is also defined by Said's through its relation to beginning: "texts," he says, "are forms of beginning and being in the world."[39]

A significant sense in which Said means beginning intention differentiates it from the way it may appear to reduce to the conscious intentions might have for a text only. In a key moment of definition, Said lays out the following:

> An intention, therefore, is a notion that includes everything that later develops out of it, no matter how eccentric the development or inconsistent the result. I do not mean, on the other hand, that intention is a more precise equivalent of totality. (Rather, they are, like the pair of terms model and paradigm, about as exactly grasped for practical literary use as a cloud. We must, however, try to be precise.) By intention I mean an appetite at the beginning intellectually to do something in a characteristic way-either consciously or unconsciously, but at any rate in a language that always (or nearly always) shows signs of the beginning intention in some form and is always engaged purposefully in the production of meaning. With regard to a given work or body of work, a beginning intention is really nothing more than the created inclusiveness within which the work develops.[40]

For Said, then, intention means the "appetite" to undertake a work of writing in a particular way and this appetite can be either conscious or unconscious in so far as it carries with it a particular shaping role. Yet the beginning intention is also something that develops over time according to a certain framing "appetite." As Said elsewhere suggests, beginning is something revisable that "implies return and repetition rather than simple linear accomplishment."[41] For Said, then, "beginning intention" as a concept, suggests an unconscious or conscious engagement with an unfolding text. And, again, the difference between origin and intention or that between beginning intention and authorial subjectivity cannot be underemphasized.

Further, beginning intention's sense of engagement seems to imply community in an indirect way, since the revisability of a text implies the many ways a text can be received and then returned to, edited, and rethought, largely before but also after entering the world (for instance through publication. And Said also opens his analysis onto the community that makes the text. "Intention," for Said, "is the link between idiosyncratic view and the communal concern."[42] This articulation, which might remind us of Glissant's sense that poetic intention bears upon "a people" withdraws the author from the antisocial position of an isolated individual (attacked even in Barthes's work). The very concept of the text being projected by the author to both the world and the critic is a reflection of this concern for textual reception within society.

THE POLITICS OF WORLD AND TEXT

In his memoir *Out of Place,* Said can be said to underplay his early awareness of the question of Palestine (though not his awareness of the related experience of exile that his family lived through in Cairo and that he did in the United States). As Brennan notes in his biography, however "[e]ven at Mt Hermon"—one of the boarding schools that he attended in the United States—"Said was already known as a passionate partisan of the Palestinian cause."[43] It is clear from sources such as Brennan's biography and Said's archived letters that he was engaged with the Palestinian question from early on and certainly as early as the late 1960s and early 1970s with which I am largely concerned. In 1969, for instance, an English professor from Gaza, Hariya Borno wrote to Said seeking assistance for opportunities in the U.S. Said would answer as he did for so many colleagues he knew through the Association of Arab-American University Graduates (AAAUG). He was constantly engaged with the question through friends such as Sami al-Banna and (perhaps most of all), the scholar and political activist Ibrahim Abu Lughod—Said's lifelong friend. And the AAAUG was a constant source of solidarity for Said's political lobbying as well as for his professional and social lives. Indeed as is well known, Said played a sustained role in staking out the position of the Palestinian Liberation Organisation despite not becoming a member. His relationship with, for instance, Yasser Arafat, went through many vicissitudes—most of all because of the stage-managed tragedy of the Oslo Accords in 1993. Whatever the case, Said was, from his earliest days, never not engaged with Palestine, with politics, and with the world.

Said's worldliness, then, was grounded from early on in his political resistance to the dispossession of the Palestinian people. Said's relationship with non-Western texts—including from the Middle East—was occasional but suggestive in this early period. The very concept of the worldly implies the relation between texts and their outside, as well as the whole-world including the East and not only the West, but the way each comes together—relatively. Consider that in *The World The Text and the Critic* Said breaks with textual hermeticism—through a critique of his colleague at Columbia, Michael Riffaterre. It is also important to note that while this book was published in 1982, its title essay appeared in print in 1976 right on the heels of *Beginnings*' release. Riffaterre had, in a recently published article in *diacritics* claimed, through a reading of Blake's poetry that "reading must be turned inwards" to the exclusion of context.[44] At any rate, Said makes this break with the view that the text is best isolated in the following way, connecting his critique of textual autonomy to the worldly:

> [M]y principal concern [in describing worldliness] is not with an aesthetic object in general, but with the text in particular. Most critics will subscribe to the notion that every literary text is in some way burdened with its occasion, with the plain empirical realities from which it emerged. Pressed too far, such a notion earns the justified criticism of a stylistician like Michel Riffaterre, who, in "The Self-Sufficient Text," calls any reduction of a text to its circumstances a fallacy, biographical, genetic, psychological, or analogic. Most critics would probably go along with Riffaterre in saying, yes, let's make sure that the text does not disappear under the weight of these fallacies. But, and here, I speak mostly for myself, they are not entirely satisfied with the idea of a self-sufficient text.[45]

Said might, here, have been writing about Barthes or Derrida (given the critique of textual autonomy), or indeed Wimsatt and Beardsley—if one alights on the word fallacy. Whatever the case, his critique of Riffaterre's emphasis on "self-sufficient" text over context would also suggest a politics of the worldly. The important thing I want to stress is that as Said came to display a certain resistance to the notion of the death or irrelevance of the author he was recommitting to a position he put to poststructuralism in *Beginnings*, he was also relating this position to the need to think alternate theories of language and signification beyond only the West. For Said, then, the rejection of the death of the author is also a move away from those modes of thought that embrace it, whether from Europe, the Middle East, or anywhere else. If this aligns with a rejection of or break with the absolute separation of author and text, this break, I suggest, is undertaken in order to open onto another (in this case, Islamic) version of the relation between text, reader, and episteme. This is why, Said, who had heretofore been given to predominantly European examples as sites to explore key critical concepts in works up to and including *Beginnings* would move in "The World, The Text, and the Critic," from Riffaterre to a mediaeval Islamic school of sacred textual interpretation.

In that essay, Said sets out several pages wherein he examines an alternate theory of language and the sign, exemplified in The Cordovan Zahirite school of interpretation, which flourished in Andalusia during the eleventh century. On the one hand, in this region of Spain at this time, there emerged another mark of interpretation championed by the Batin school. As Said explains, differentiating the two schools:

> Batinists held that meaning in language is concealed within the words; meaning is therefore available only as the result of an inward-tending exegesis. The Zahirites—their name derives from the Arabic word for clear, apparent, and phenomenal; Batin connotes internal—argued that words had only a surface meaning, one that was anchored to a particular usage, circumstance, historical and religious situation.[46]

Said develops this distinction, which may now begin to appear both august—even ancient—and yet familiar, since it figures the kinds of debates in textual meaning and its location that were raging in the contemporary moment and into which he intervened. Said continues: "The Cordovan Zahirites attacked the excesses of the Batinists, arguing that the very profession of grammar (in Arabic *nahu*) was an invitation to spinning out private meanings in an otherwise divinely pronounced, and hence unchangeably stable, text."[47] As such, Said lays out the distinction between the Batinists and the Zahirites as a distinction between the former's emphasis on textual autonomy (giving rise to potentially wider interpretation subsequently) and a contextually located methodology— one that delimits potential interpretation and was favored by the Zahirites. Given the critique of Riffaterre that this discussion follows (and much else in his work as we have seen), it is clear, Said prefers the Zahirites. Said, would elaborate further:

> The Zahirite effort was to restore by rationalization a system of reading a text in which attention was focused on the phenomenal words themselves, in what might be considered their once-and-for-all sense uttered for and during a specific occasion, not on hidden meanings they might later be supposed to contain. The Cordovan Zahirites in particular went very far in trying to provide a reading system that placed the tightest possible control over the reader and his circumstances. They did this principally by means of a theory of what a text is.[48]

For Said, an important lesson of the Zahirite school and "what ought to strike us forcibly about the whole theory is that it represents a considerably articulated thesis for dealing with a text as a significant form." Further, this form emphasizes:

> worldliness, circumstantiality, the text's status as an event having sensuous particularity as well as historical contingency, are consider as being incorporated in the test's status as an event having sensuous particularity as well as historical contingency, are considered as being incorporated in the text, an infrangible part of its capacity for conveying and producing meaning. This means that a text has a specific situation, placing restraints upon the interpreter and his interpretation not because the situation is hidden within the text as a mystery, but rather because the situation exists at the same level of surface particularity as the textual object itself.[49]

This analytic observation should lead us to the conclusion that Said's refusal of the strictly textual operation of the structuralists and poststructuralists (or much of their thought) is also grounded in his emphasis on worldliness. Clearly Said's implicit provocation is not only to suggest that context needs to complement textual analysis but he is also suggesting this is not a new debate, subtly passing judgment on the ridiculousness of a twentieth-century thinker who might think such a provocation novel. Yet, Said was hardly rejecting diligent textual analysis—his account of the text through Piaget and Foucault is one example of his taking this practice thoroughly seriously. Rather Said's examination of the Cordovites' emphasis on "usage, circumstance, historical and religious situation" suggests another thought, from beyond the West, foregrounding the context's capacity to open the phenomenology of language. And while the Cordovites favored context in the sense of that which is common to the contemporary (not unlike, of course, the much later Cambridge school, Said's embrace of them seems not so narrow but representative of a wider concern with the contextualization of hermeneutic interpretation. It is appropriate that the root of a theory of worldliness comes from a non-Western text even as Said demonstrably saw openness to the world, juxtaposed with groundedness in one's context everywhere.

Said's analysis of textual context of course drew on contemporary methods (and from his own pragmatic attitude). His gesture to medieval Islam was a gesture to non-Western knowledge. And indeed, he would close out the essay exploring the materiality and linguistic phenomenology of the colonial situation through a pointed use of Frantz Fanon's ideas. Quoting at length Fanon's account in *The Wretched of the Earth* of the unequal architectural distribution of power and access of the colonial situation:

> The zone where the natives live is not complementary to the zone inhabited by the settlers. The two zones are opposed, but not in the service of a higher unity . . . The settlers' town is a strongly-built town, all made of stone and steel . . . The town belonging to the colonized people, or at least the native town, the negro village, the medina, the reservation, is a place of ill fame, peopled by men of evil repute. They are born there, it matters little where or how; they die there, it matters not where, nor how.[50]

Said draws on this moment in Fanon to reflect on the active response to a concrete colonial situation—material as well as linguistic, indeed, material because linguistic, which is to say discursive. The material suffering of colonized people is, for Said, engendered by discourse: "No wonder that the Fanonist solution to such discourse is violence."[51] What could be said to attract Said to Fanon is not only the latter's active resistance to colonization but the mode of this resistance that connects its materiality to its grasp of language and the symbolic. This is the same thing that differentiated Foucault from Derrida to Said in 1978; Said in spite of his skepticism about poststructuralism continues to be attracted to modes of thought that tie discursive critiques of power to the materiality which that mode of thought manifests. He would make these connections as such in his 1975 interview:

> To reintegrate himself with worldly actuality, the critic of texts ought to be investigating the system of discourse by which the "world" is divided, administered, plundered, by which humanity is thrust into pigeon-holes, by which "we" are "human" and "they" are not, and so forth We will discover that even so innocuous a discipline as philology has played a crucial role in this process. Most important, we should be intent upon revealing the secrecy, the privatisations of texts whose circumstantial thickness and complicity are covered by the otherworldly prestige of art or of "mere" textuality.[52]

The critic of text is, then, nothing without a sense of the world and of the way human beings are divided within it. For Said, there is no adequate sense of the textual without a sense of the material and with it, of the world. Yet this sense of the material is also related to the will—to the agential act of the imagination in and on this world.

Empire and Intention

As time wore on, Said would increasingly elaborate a sense of text and context that insisted on situating textual play in the world, connected to sociopolitical conviction and, importantly grounded in at least some sense of what conviction is: an intention. As such the role of intention could be situated in at least two ways for Said: without intention, power could not be held to account and, from another angle, without intention, genius could not be held up as such. By the time of 1993's *Culture and Imperialism*, Said would find both complicity with great colonial violence within works whose genius he would also acknowledge.[53] From the West Indian source of Rochester's fortunes in *Jane Eyre* to the French Imperialist designs over Algeria hidden within Camus' universalism, Said would, in that book, reveal the relation between power, intention, and empire. Yet there would be no figure who better animated the complexities of Empire, for Said, than Joseph Conrad.

Early on in *Culture and Imperialism*, Said suggests that *Heart of Darkness* offers two simultaneous visions of Empire. The first is the blunt instrument of Imperial power—the rough edged violence and brutality of (for instance) Leopold in the Belgian Congo. As Said puts it, this first vision or argument:

> allows the old imperial enterprise full scope to play itself out conventionally, to render the world as official European or Western imperialism saw it, and to consolidate itself after World War Two. Westerners may have physically left their old colonies in Africa and Asia, but they retained them not only as markets but as locales on the ideological map over which they continued to rule morally and intellectually.[54]

As Said continues, this entitled logic of Empire blames the colonized person and people for the moral failings encountered in his territory.

> The assertions of this discourse exclude what has been represented as "lost" by arguing that the colonial world was in some ways ontologically speaking lost to begin with, irredeemable, irrecusably inferior. Moreover, it focusses

not on what was shared in the colonial experience, but on what must never be shared, namely the authority and rectitude that come with greater power and development.[55]

This sense of inferiority is, no doubt, the source of the racist vision of Africa and Africans that many, (though perhaps most notably, Chinua Achebe), have identified in Conrad's novella.[56] Yet, as Said points out, there is also a sustained critique of Empire that emerges in *Heart of Darkness* and it is this critique that makes possible the second of the two visions he sees there. As Said says, it is not only the case that there is a great deal of criticism of Empire in Conrad's prose that leads us to the sense that he sees not inevitability but agency in the experience of the colonized, it is also the contingency of Empire itself that is so emphasized in (for instance) Marlowe's conjuring of Roman Britain. As Said suggests,

> Since Conrad *dates* imperialism, shows its contingency, records its illusions and tremendous violence and waste (as in *Nostromo*), he permits his later readers to imagine something other than an Africa carved up into dozens of European colonies, even if, for his own part, he had little notion of what that Africa might be.[57]

Implicit in this notion is the idea that the liberation struggles he names in a page or so ("Algeria, Cuba, Vietnam, Palestine, Iran" and of course the decolonization of Africa) were not only enabled by the contingency of empire (though they were) but also by the agency of those participating in the varying forms of resistance.

I want to make two further observations, not the least since my recapitulation of Said's sense of there being two visions in *Heart of Darkness* is fairly uncontroversial on its own. The first is to note that at the precise moment Said makes his doubled case about ways of reading Conrad, he turns to the kind of critique of contemporary theory that he had, we have seen, increasingly turned to through the 1970s and 1980s. Said critiques Jean-Francois Lyotard and Foucault as examples of poststructuralist theory's turn away from the critique of power toward other, perhaps more insular, ends. In both, he sees warning cases in the emphasis on the futility of resistance to power in those spaces named above. Of Foucault, he notes:

> Foucault [. . .] turned his attention away from the oppositional forces in modern society which he had studied for their undeterred resistance to exclusion and confinement--delinquents, poets, outcasts, and the like—and decided that since power was everywhere it was probably better to concentrate on the local micro-physics of power that surround the individual. The self was therefore to be studied, cultivated, and, if necessary, refashioned and constituted.[58]

Foucault's later work on ethics and the "care of the self," then, comes to stand, for Said, for depoliticization. And theory more generally came to be seen as crestfallen, winded, and given to a refusal of politics, agency, and resistance—the same things Said's emphasis on intention were supposed to retain in the literary realm.

It was to a literary term that Said would also turn in order to identify this depoliticization in the work of the two French poststructuralists:

> In both Lyotard and Foucault we find precisely the same trope employed to explain the disappointment in the politics of liberation: narrative, which posits an enabling beginning point and a vindicating goal, is no longer adequate for plotting the human trajectory in society.[59]

For Said, this sense of narrative—the grand narrative of Lyotard, for instance—circumscribes agency where narrative was once a means of attaining it. Narrative here stands for the prescribed and determined as opposed to the agency emergent from a beginning intention. Interestingly, ten or so years earlier, Said (again with Conrad in mind) considered the mode of that author's "presentation of narrative." In an essay of that name it was precisely the relation between telling and being told (literal narration) that animated the storytelling capacity the author designs to capture. As Said noted:

> [i]nterestingly, the dramatic protocol of much of Conrad's fiction is the swapped yarn, the historical report, the mutually exchanged legend, the musing recollection. This protocol implies (although often they are explicitly there) a speaker and a hearer and, as I said earlier, sometimes a specific enabling occasion.[60]

We can be put in mind of the telling of stories in *Lord Jim* here, or indeed, of Marlowe on the Nellie in *Heart of Darkness*, to name only several of many possible examples. Of Conrad's interest in oral communication, Said makes much and apart from much else, he emphasizes the capacity for Conrad's narrative style to address the transmission of an intention (or at least, the representation of this transmission). As Said puts it, a page later, Conrad wishes to delve into a "realm of vision beyond the words":

> There, rifts in the community of man or in the damaged ego are healed, and the space separating ambition from activity is narrowed. Retrospective time and events are corrected for divergences. Or, still more radically, the writer's intention of wishing to say something very clearly is squared completely with the reader's seeing; by the labors of a solitary writer, words affixed to the page become the common unmediated property of the reader, who penetrates past the words to their author's visual intention, which is the same as his written-presentation.[61]

For Said, Conrad then, attempted at replicating the "yarn," or the "legend"—storytelling as such beyond the written word, giving the vivid sense of character and agency to the fictional tellers (and, perhaps the implied author capturing these storytelling capacities). What does the Conrad of narrative Said sees have to do with the Conrad whom Said sees as deploying two visions of Empire? I would suggest that it is narrative in its unrestricted, intentionalist sense that makes it possible for Said to detect both Imperialism and its critique in Conrad's complex work. For the neoconservatives (one thinks of Francis Fukuyama or Samuel Huntington) and, both ironically and unfortunately, for some tendencies of poststructuralism, narrative foreclosed agency—as Said put it of Foucault and Lyotard, "[t]here is nothing to look forward to; we are stuck within our circle. And now the line is enclosed by a circle."[62] What was dynamic, for Said, in the reading of literature such for instance as in Conrad was the opening of such circles, the agency of the author and reader as storyteller and listener. Of course, what emerges is both Conrad the anti-Imperialist and Conrad the racist.

Said's critique of Foucault in *Culture and Imperialism* was also vested in a comparison to a figure he would by then prefer and whom we have met before: Fanon. Late in the text, Said writes of an "instructive reminder" in the comparison between the two.[63] Said drew the distinction, emphasizing that,

Fanon's work programmatically seeks to treat colonial and metropolitan societies together, as discrepent but related entities, while Foucault's work moves further and further away from serious consideration of social wholes, focusing instead upon the individual as dissolved in the ineluctably advancing 'microphysics of power' that it is hopeless to resist. Fanon represents the interests of a double constituency, native and Western, moving from confinement to liberation; ignoring the imperial context of his own theories, Foucault seems actually to represent an irresistible colonizing movement that paradoxically fortifies the prestige of both the lonely individual scholar and the system that contains him.[64]

We would seem to be far from the younger Said here, corresponding, as we saw with Foucault himself. In *Orientalism*—his most influential work—Said appears to have vested much of his method in one derived from discursive analysis and Foucault. Neil Lazarus in both refusing the characterization of *Orientalism* as "Foucauldian" and also the counter-weighted characterization of the book as only superficially invested in Foucault to assert that, "Foucault's work provides a central point of departure, and of reference, for Said in *Orientalism*."[65] Did these bold declarations in *Culture and Imperialism* carry with them, ironically, an epistemic break. I think not. As I have been sketching, since as early as *Beginnings* and the essays it compiled, Said already brought to bear on discourse as a topos also the force of a sensibility associated with agency and humanism as I have begun to suggest. And as Anthony Alessandrini has suggested, this forceful sense of agency was not nostalgic or "residual," in Raymond Williams' sense, but decidedly forward-looking and emergent.

The turn in Said to defend what Alessandrini has usefully termed Said's "emergent humanism" would intensify in a 1994 afterword to *Orientalism*.[66] Said noted that "among American and British academics of a decidedly rigorous and unyielding stripe," Orientalism had been attacked not for its ostensibly monolithic account of the West (though that had been one line of attack) but for the "residual humanism" it bolstered; this was particularly objectionable in an era of dominance for what the Anglo-American academy tended to call postmodern theory (with its emphasis on structure over agency).[67] Said, noted that his book had been slighted for its apparent, "theoretical inconsistencies, its insufficient, perhaps even sentimental, treatment of agency."[68] His response was to declare his emphasis on agency a deliberate and necessary step, immediately continuing:

I am glad that it has! *Orientalism* is a partisan book, not a theoretical machine. No one has convincingly shown that individual effort is not at some profoundly unteachable level both eccentric and, in Gerard Manley Hopkins's sense *original*; this despite the existence of systems of thought, discourses, harmonies, (although none of them are in fact seamless, perfect, or inevitable).[69]

Here once again, Said implicitly refuses to abandon the "discourses," structures, and harmonies that had lent analytical consistency to analysis like *Orientalism*. Yet Said also emphasizes the power of partisan analysis, the degree to which the human and the author can agentially withstand subordination to system only. Alessandrini hones in on Said's response to anthropologist James Clifford's critique of his apparently "totalizing" humanism, Said's humanism, in being engaged with the antihumanist structuralisms refused the essentialist narrative of the human species, culture, and life.[70] In this way Said's humanism was not residual but emergent. In Said's own words, "I did not (and still do not) see in humanism only the kind of totalizing and essentializing trends that Clifford identifies."[71] He instead believed "one could fashion a different kind of humanism."[72] Said had passed through the practice of discursive critique and the high intentionalist form of thinking the human and what emerges within his thought is this emergent humanism, aware of the workings of discourses and structures on the human mind but not willing to allow a similarly totalizing structuralism that refused to acknowledge human capacity to resist, however desperately and even with futility the operations of power upon them. This maneuver is nowhere more apparent than when Said rethinks authorship to both maintain his own signature and imprimatur on the work and yet to acknowledge a "much-expanded sense of authorship that goes well beyond the egoism of the solitary beings we feel ourselves to be as we undertake a piece of work." He declared *Orientalism* a "collective book that I think supersedes me as an author more than I could have expected when I wrote it."[73] The author was here to lose himself in the labyrinthine structures that produced him, but only to emerge once more to acknowledge simultaneously his subjectivity alongside his conditioning by culture and structure.

The intervention of authorship is not necessarily virtuous but is thoroughly agential and—among other consequences—can, thus, be held accountable. Said's account of both the imprint of the beginning moment of intention and recognition of the collective enterprise that authorship can be, bespeaks the "link between idiosyncratic view and the communal concern" that he himself began with many years before. The way authorship relates itself and turns toward the community from which it arises is a function of storytelling itself.

Notes

1. Timothy Brennan, *Places of Mind: A Life of Edward Said*. London: Bloomsbury, 2021, 97.
2. Roland Barthes to Edward Said, 25 August 1972 Edward Said Papers MS 1524. Box 5, Folder 2.
3. Edward Said, "Michel Foucault as an Intellectual Imagination," in *Boundary 2*, 1, 1 (1972): 1–36.
4. Michel Foucault to Edward Said, 5 November 1972. Edward Said Papers MS 1524. Box 5, Folder 3.
5. Roland Barthes to Edward Said, 11 November 1972. Edward Said Papers MS 1524. Box 5, Folder 5.
6. Said, "Diary: My Encounter with Sartre," in *London Review of Books*, 22, 11 (2000). https://www.lrb.co.uk/the-paper/v22/n11/edward-said/diary.
7. Brennan, *Places of Mind*, 235.
8. Brennan, *Places of Mind*, 219.
9. Key scholars in the last twenty years have made this point, calling attention to the misleading nature of the claim that Said is purely and simply a Foucauldian. As well as Anthony Alessandrini's *Frantz Fanon and the Future of Cultural Politics*, this idea has been explored by Mathieu E. Courvlle in his "Genealogies of Postcolonialism: A Slight Return from Said and Foucault Back to Fanono and Sartre," in *Studies in Religion/Scences Religieuses* 36, 2 (2007): 215–240.
10. Said, "Diary."
11. Brennan, *Places of Mind*, 175.
12. Joseph Massad, "Sartre, European Intellectuals and Zionism," *The Electronic Intifada*, 31 January 2003.
13. Edward Said to Michel Foucault, 15 January 1973. Edward Said Papers MS 1524. Box 5, Folder 4. Author's translation.
14. Edward Said to Michel Foucault, 15 January 1973. Edward Said Papers MS 1524. Box 5, Folder 4. Author's translation.

15. Edward Said to Michel Foucault, 15 January 1973. Edward Said Papers MS 1524. Box 5, Folder 4.
16. Said, *Beginnings*, 191.
17. Said, "The Problem of Textuality: Two Exemplary Positions" in *Critical Inquiry* 4, 4 (1978): 673–714, 700. Literal translations from the French original added in square parentheses by the author.
18. Said, *The World, The Text and the Critic*. Cambridge, MA: Harvard University Press, 1983. The book was originally to have been named "Methods." See Brennan, *Places of Mind*, 225.
19. Edward Said to Erwin A. Glikes, 20 March 1973, Edward Said Papers MS 1524. Box 5, Folder 5.
20. Edward Said to Monroe Engel, 28 June 1973, Edward Said Papers MS 1524. Box 5, Folder 6.
21. Said to Engel, 28 June 1973.
22. Said to Engel, 28 June 1973.
23. Edward Said, "Beginnings," in *Power, Politics and Culture: Interviews with Edward Said*. London: Bloomsbury, 2004, 18.
24. Said, "Beginnings," in *Power, Politics and Culture*, 24.
25. Brennan, *Places of Mind*, 231.
26. Said *Beginnings: Intention and Method*. London: Granta, 1985 [1975] 3, xxiii, 23, 83–84.
27. Said, *Beginnings*, 6.
28. Said, *Beginnings*, xxiii.
29. Said, *Beginnings*, 218.
30. Said, *Beginnings*, 373.
31. Said, *Beginnings*, 373, original emphasis.
32. Said, *Reflections on Exile and Other Essays*, Cambridge, MA: Harvard, 2000, 173.
33. Glissant, *Poetics of Relation*, 7.
34. Said, *Reflections on Exile*, 186.
35. Said, *Beginnings*, 361.
36. Said, *Beginnings*, 174.
37. Said, *Beginnings*, 23.
38. Said, *Beginnings*, xxi.
39. Said, *Beginnings*, xxii.
40. Said, *Beginnings*, 12.
41. Said, *Beginnings*, xxiii.
42. Said, *Beginnings*, 13.

43. Brennan, *Places of Mind*, 40.
44. Michael Riffaterre, "The Self-Sufficient Text," in *Diacritics* 3, 3 (1973): 39–45, 40.
45. Said, *The World, The Text and the Critic*, 35.
46. Said, *The World, The Text and the Critic*, 36.
47. Said, *The World, The Text and the Critic*, 36.
48. Said, *The World, The Text and the Critic*, 37.
49. Said, *The World, The Text and the Critic*, 37.
50. Quoted in Said, *The World, The Text and the Critic*, 49.
51. Said, *The World, The Text and the Critic*, 49.
52. Said, "Beginnings," in *Power, Politics and Culture*, 26.
53. Said, *Culture and Imperialism*. New York. Vintage, 1994.
54. Said, *Culture and Imperialism*, 25.
55. Said, *Culture and Imperialism*, 25.
56. Chinua Achebe, "An Image of Africa: Racism in Conrad's 'Heart of Darkness.'" in *The Massachusetts Review*, 18 (1977).
57. Said, *Culture and Imperialism*, 26.
58. Said, *Culture and Imperialism*, 26.
59. Said, *Culture and Imperialism*, 26–27.
60. Said, *The World, The Text and the Critic*, 94.
61. Said, *The World, The Text and the Critic*, 95.
62. Said, *Culture and Imperialism*, 27.
63. Said, *Culture and Imperialism*, 335.
64. Said, *Culture and Imperialism*, 335–336.
65. Lazarus, *The Postcolonial Unconscious*, 188.
66. Alessandrini, *Frantz Fanon and the Future of Cultural Politics*, 62.
67. Said, *Orientalism* (1994), 339.
68. Said, *Orientalism* (1994), 339.
69. Said, *Orientalism* (1994), 339.
70. Said makes his defence against Clifford in the former's *Humanism and Democratic Criticism*. New York: Columbia University Press, 2003.
71. Said, *Humanism and Democratic Criticism*, 10.
72. Said, *Humanism and Democratic Criticism*, 10.
73. Said, *Orientalism* (1994), 330.

CHAPTER 5

On Writing, Storytelling, Community

Abstract In order to examine another potential conception of authorship, this final conclusive chapter departs from a key observation: If Barthes was right about the relation between authorship and capitalism in the Global North, it was not necessarily the case in the Global South. The chapter follows a pointed line of thought, amounting to less a simplistic rejection of the death of the author and more an attendant question: what are the consequences of this critique of authorship for the anticolonial storyteller? If the (liberal, capitalist) author is dead, what is the meaning of this figure's rebirth for storytelling? The chapter examines more recent scholarship for critical conceptions of storytelling that emphasize presence and even ritual over the static figure of the individual author-genius associated by Barthes with European enlightenment and capitalism. Finally the chapter asks through the diverse cast of characters the book has been calling on throughout: What are the political consequences of a rethought version of the author and their agency?

Keywords Anticolonial thought · Decolonization · Storytelling Sylvia Wynter · Kamau Brathwaite

Recall that Barthes began with the distinction between, on the one hand, "a mediator, shaman or relator whose 'performance'—the mastery of the narrative code—may possibly be admired but never his 'genius'" and, on the other, the modern figure of the author, whose genius centers any account of inventiveness and agency.[1] Throughout this book, I have explored the various ways such figures of anticolonial thought as Fanon, Said, and Glissant were significantly engaged with the question of the author from the earliest moments in the reception of the idea of this figure's "death." As we saw in my first chapter, before Barthes' argument had effected the transformation it (no doubt) effected, a number of figures such as Wilson Harris and Frantz Fanon had already begun to produce an account of authorship: one wedded more to action and community than to the bourgeois self that would come to be Barthes' target. If Barthes was right about the relation between authorship and capitalism in the Global North, it was not necessarily the case in the Global South. So, it is crucial to ask: how might authorship be thought of as given to a collective decolonial enterprise rather than as necessarily a bourgeois vestige of capitalist individualism, as Barthes saw it?

In his recent book, *Racism and "Free Speech,"* Anshuman Mondal draws out a pointed deconstruction of liberal principles such as free speech—including the degree to which these principles rely on an internalized emphasis on abstracted notions of individualism (many of which are derived from market principles). Mondal articulates a key stake of his argument as follows:

> liberalism's conceptualization of 'free speech' is determined by a prior and continuing investment by liberalism in an *inequality* that is obscured by a merely formal equality between abstracted and disembodied 'individuals' that is accompanied by an emphasis on purely procedural frameworks that are supposed to be neutral.[2]

While my argument is not about free speech as such but in its form as creative expression, I take a cue from Mondal's emphasis on the abstracted, disembodied individual who comes to represent the subject of enunciation for free, creative expression. This was emphasized by Barthes indirectly in his own critique of the modern figure of the author and yet, whether through an emphasis on the *quimboiseur* or through a more expansive secular humanism, those who approached authorship differently also, in novel ways rejected the author as reducible to a subject of liberal individualism. What this book has amounted to is less a simplistic rejection of the death of the author and more an attendant question: What are the consequences of this critique of authorship for the anticolonial storyteller? If the (liberal, capitalist) author is dead, what is the meaning of this figure's rebirth for storytelling?

There is an irony in the fact that a figure most firmly associated with the Global North (metropolitan Paris), Barthes, emphasizes and validates the figure of the shaman, in its slippage with other terms of storytelling ("relator," "mediator") while Said, we can easily assume would not have gone in for any of the mystical connotations aligned with shamanism; Said was situated in secular storytelling. Glissant, himself preferred the figure of the *quimboiseur*, arguably an equally secular keeper of lore and history. Indeed, the notion of the shaman is perhaps as much a projection of modernity on the precolonial figure of various kinds of storyteller and even clever person as anything else. Nonetheless, I want to explore here how storytelling, in a newly refabulated way might be a productive emergent logic of the death of the author after its critique by anticolonial figures such as those compassed in this book.

As we have seen in the remainder of this book, scholars such as Glissant and Said were, after 1967, subtly critical of Barthes' rejection of authorial agency tout court, forming alternative conceptions of what it means to write. However, just as Barthes drew this distinction forcefully between the figure of the author-genius and that of the shaman mediator, many thinkers to follow would engage with the theory of the literary (and for that matter, the oral) tradition in such a way as to offer novel interpellations of each of these two figures and of their relation.

If Barthes is right and the shaman/mediator is valued for the mastery of a given "narrative code" over a genius for the original, then it may be on this point that critics from the Global South (or many of them), might follow him. The contention of this short book has not been so much that anticolonial writers are necessarily on the side of literary intentionalism—or at least not in any simplistic way. After all, Glissant's notion of poetic intention, as we saw, was also deeply connected to relation and an expansive embrace of otherness, as well as connection and community; Said's notion of a beginning intention, included within it the elaborations to follow it, their idiosyncrasies and the "communal concern" they entailed. Neither author subscribed to a reinscription of the capitalist figure of the author defaced by Barthes and yet Glissant, at least, in his wider project did not reject the figure of the *quimboiseur* or the storyteller. Decolonial writers do not necessarily subscribe to literary intentionalism, or related approaches to authorship which do not refuse presence *tout court* just as it is not the case that white writers necessarily reject it (consider on this last point the work of Walter Benn Michaels who insists on the political salience of intentionalism to emphasize economic inequality, though often over the salience of race and gender). Nor is it the case that intentionalism is necessarily liberatory (consider for example the example of philosopher Kathleen Stock and her attempt to recoup authorial intention for ultimately conservative ends).[3] Indeed, while literary intentionalism may seem on the face of it to have little to do with politics and this is so in spite of studies of the relation between such literary theoretical concerns and Marxist political commitments being shown to be thick and considerable as they have by such figures as Michaels. The contention this book has explored with emphasis on the examples given by Glissant and Said is that from the moment Barthes made his provocation that the author is dead, giving rise to "the birth of the reader," there emerged powerful anticolonial perspectives on this evocative notion. Indeed, as I have suggested about Harris and Fanon, a few voices had already emerged that would articulate an alternative mode of thinking authorship and community *avant la lettre*.

How the sense of Said's notion of orientalism as a discourse of power and knowledge would impact related fields of study (such as postcolonial studies but also black and Indigenous studies, for instance) presents numerous pathways. One very direct one took place in November of 1978, not long after *Orientalism*'s release. That month, a scholar at Union Theological Seminary sent Said a handwritten letter extolling the book's virtues and suggesting where its ideas might have been pushed further. The scholar—who would rise to be greatly admired in his own right—Cornel West drew on his background in African-American studies, philosophy, and theology to suggest that he, as a reader and thinker, "would have liked to see a bit more about the response of coloured peoples to the hegemonic cultural will to power of Western Imperialism."[4] West's critique was vested in the agency of those undertaking resistance. He elaborated:

> [a]s you say, one audience (among others) of your book is third world peoples who should be reminded that they are up against a strong hegemonic culture. But isn't it possible that what you so accurately describe and account for may have a paralyzing effect on oppressed peoples? That is, for political and ideological persons, some space may have been apportioned

for critical opposition (like your own work and writings of [Egyptian-French political theorist] Anwar Abdel-Malek) among *organic intellectuals* and "common folk."⁵

What I find striking here is the way this early response to *Orientalism* by an intellectual of great power and presence was making of Said the very criticisms the latter had attempted to bring to bear (so very politely) against Foucault five or six years before. Where Said had put in place a series of caveats to the centering of analysis on discourse—caveats from agency and beginning intention—West's analysis would bring home the degree to which Said's work had strayed from these declared commitments to instead tarry too sustainedly with Foucauldian methodology in even as masterful a study as *Orientalism*. West was not the only scholar making connections between black and Palestinian liberation. A few years later, Ernest J. Wilson would write, reviewing *Orientalism*,

> The "Palestinian problem" is now before the entire world for resolution. It is not just a local struggle. The resolution of the Black liberation struggle will have international as well as local significance, not only for Blacks but for the United States as a whole, and hence the entire international community.⁶

Orientalism would, it seems, be a springboard to many and varied international solidarities in resistance, even as West's critique remained salient—an elaboration in the spirit of Said's own project. Wilson's detailed review of Said's book took such solidarities as his basis and departure point. If the critique of these discourses was to matter at all, it was to matter in so far as it avowed the "liberation struggles" of Palestinian and other oppressed peoples—and the solidarities attendant on them. Critique was only the beginning, liberation was the ultimate outcome that Wilson sought in Said's work.

Said's articulation of discursive power in the sense of orientalism was inspirational to some, a paradigm to be extended for others. Just as West emphasized the need for Said to return to the agency and action that the latter had himself championed, so scholars engaging with Glissant would identify comparable and also inverse paradigms. Sylvia Wynter, writing in 1990, would, ironically vest her case—an intricate and expansive one—in a comparison between Glissant's project and Foucault's famous prognostication of the erasure of the figure of man, washed away "like a face drawn in sand at the edge of the sea."[7] For Wynter, the dispersion of the enlightenment figure of man was not only a construction that could, as Foucault had seen it, transform European conceptions of subjectivity (like the figure of man to be erased). This project also bore consequences for the specific articulation of individual agential projects in the global South, with relation to blackness and with the Caribbean specifically at stake for Glissant. Wynter writes:

> The specificity of the problem particular and unique to the Antilles was and is therefore an existential one, in that in order to attain to optimal being on the model of secular Man, to attain to being human, the Antillean subject had to be against not only the specificity of its own physiognomic being (Cesaire, Fanon) and the specificity of its own Antillean kinship based on the "peculiarity of its own history" as the only people who had been denied human status (Cesaire), but, as Glissant will further develop and extend, to the specificity of its own Creole language, of its own landscape and lived existential history, the specificity of that to which Glissant gives name, of its Antilleanity.[8]

What is at stake here for Wynter is to open poststructural analysis (and Foucault is her focus) to the terrain it arguably avoids: the specificity of varying struggles for anticolonial liberation. Not only that, but Wynter sees this logical but (for the poststructuralists, largely) untrodden consequence emerge in two key topoi: first as part of a wider decolonial critical tradition—Cesaire and Fanon are mentioned here, but she earlier parses also George Lamming and Maryse Condé.[9] Second, it is through the specific linguistic practices of colonized people in which Glissant (and Wynter) see a heterogenous range of practices, with an emphasis on such modes of communication as forced poetics/counterpoetics and Creole. These poetic and linguistic practices go beyond the word of man and, I would suggest, beyond the genius of the author, to produce something we might see as a craft of writing that could take on not so much the mysticism of shamanism as the lore of the quimboiseur. Writing, then, becomes not a practice of the individual but, through Creole and related forms, a practice of opening to the enunciator's community. And, as we have seen, to begin with intention and presence and move to community eventually bears, for Glissant on a relation with what he called the Whole-world.

Figures from decolonizing and postcolonial backgrounds each, in their own way, link the question of the author and her or his intentions to their place in the community. The Caribbean has been importantly and uniquely at the forefront of this articulation (though not, I hasten to add, being the only community to articulate the relation between language, intention, and community vis a vis Creole and the like). Recall, as I did in my introduction, that Wilson Harris, as early as 1967 and independently of Barthes, emphasized the position of the writer not in relation to the abstract condition of "man" or "humanity" and rather in relation to the "truth of community: "the writer—the 'creative' writer at whom we have been looking—both transcends and undermines (or deepens if you will) the mode of society since the truth of community which he pursues is not a self-evident fact: it is neither purely circumscribed nor purely produced by economic circumstance."[10] Again we see the role of the community in relation to which the author composes as essential to this subversion that Barthes saw as essential for the "modern" figure of the author—a genius in a vacuum.

Like Harris, Barbadian author Kamau Brathwaite had a contribution to make to understanding of the relation between individual expression and the community. Further, his emphasis lay on the sound or, as he terms it "noise" in poetry. For Brathwaite, orality is central to the account of the way languages mix and combine, creolize, and also (crucially for a black Caribbean intellectual) bear the presences of African languages within colonial ones—what he calls "Nation language."[11] As he says in his 1984 lecture *History of the Voice*, Brathwaite suggests that "[t]he poetry, the culture itself" of Nation language "exists not in the dictionary but in the tradition of the spoken word."[12] He continues

> It is based on sound as much as it is on song. That is to say, the noise that it makes is part of the meaning, and if you ignore the noise (or what you *think* of as noise, shall I say) then you lose part of the meaning. When it is written, you lose the sound or the noise and therefore you lose part of the meaning.[13]

As we saw in my second chapter with Senghor and Glissant, Brathwaite is interested in the relation between the signified (the sound-image) as bearer of meaning, including sound (or "noise"). Importantly, where noise is often dismissed as incidental or accidental, Brathwaite insists on landing on the accidence of the accidental. What "you *think* of as noise" is in fact able to be yoked to the project of the storyteller. In asserting the importance of noise and storytelling in this way, Brathwaite must come to the figure of the African and Caribbean teller of tales: the griot. He introduces the figure in this way:

> The other thing about nation language is that it is part of what might be called *total expression*, a notion which is not unfamiliar to you because you are coming back to that kind of thing now. Reading is an isolated, individualistic expression. The oral tradition on the other hand demands not only the griot but the audience to complete the community: the noise and sounds that the maker makes are responded to by the audience and are returned to him. Hence we have the creation of a continuum where meaning truly resides.[14]

By emphasizing the role of the audience, Brathwaite—like Glissant, who the former also cites—emphasizes the interdependency of poetic intention given in the intentional and adapted to articulations that appear as noise. In doing so, poetic intention comes to rely on the audience and the griot, therefore only holding an intention in so far as they reinvest in the community that are their addressees.

There remains the question of the scope and extent of the community in question. Do expressions of resistance such as those given in what Glissant calls "forced poetics" or "counterpoetics," as we saw in Chapter 2 and those which Brathwaite calls "nation language" come from one community? How far does that community reach? What is the specificity of each mode of decolonizing resistance, be it black, say, or, Caribbean in particular, or Palestinian (or otherwise)? And indeed, is there *one* black mode of resistance, *one* Palestinian way of being that seeks to offer resistance and the promise of decolonization or, on the other hand, many? What could this articulation of the heterogeneity and specificity of struggle have to do with the decolonization of the death of the author? It is precisely the limitations of homogenization that are questioned by any emphasis on the ipseity of a speaking position, whether of a writer or their community. As Wynter writes of Glissant,

> If we make use of Foucault's distinction between an intelligentsia that defines itself as the bearer of a "just-and-true-for-all" truth and the "specific intellectual" as one who works not in the name of a universal—i.e., liberal nationalism, Marxism, and/or feminism—but rather as on the terrain and in the mode of struggle provided by the existential conditions of her or his life to which she or he bears witness, with these conditions defining the specific nature of what that intellectual struggle must be, it is clear

[for Glissant] that it is only where the terrain of struggle has been that of being that the Antillean intellectuals have reenacted the empirical struggles of the popular forces at the level of ideas and of imaginative discourse.[15]

For Wynter, in her parsing of Glissant, then, struggle must ground itself in the specificity of a time and place—of a community. Similarly, for African-American feminist scholar Hortense Spillers, the risk of homogenization is a telling one. For Spillers, there is not one but there are rather multiple ways of articulating black culture, indeed, "black cultures"—and they should be pluralized—are, for Spillers, divided precisely by such a situation as we have been describing by thinking about the figure of the modern author rethought in Glissant and, differently Brathwaite's terms as *quimboiseur* or *griot*. Spillers suggests:

> The diasporic cultures in question, then, have been summoned to unmake the conditions of alienation, simultaneous with the actual exploiting the force of it in order to make new, to bring into existence a repertoire of predicates that were not there before so far as we can see. Since we cannot easily separate these imperatives from each other, we would have to say that New World black cultures, as well as their parallel formations in other parts of the globe, are not only Creole forms adopted from the implements, both material and imaginative, of the near-at-hand, but that they are also "schizophrenic," if by that we mean compounded of a disposition that carries both its statement and counterstatement, that would both undo alienation and constitute its own standpoint.[16]

Could it be, then, that in order to maintain the critique of the figure of the modern author after Barthes's declaration of his demise, the question of the relative heterogeneity of the addressee (the community) is a vital one? This would mean a modern instantiation of the *griot* or *quimboiseur* would be aware of many communities but address themselves to the specificity of the one they aim to reach, as was the case in Glissant's forced poetics, the speaker for Spillers is schizophrenic in this understanding, divided against himself. Spillers however sees this as a turning away, but also a move toward the real. Limning W. E. B. DuBois, she suggests:

> "Spirit" across this canon was both the retreat, the "oasis," from the commercial impulses of mainstream civilization at the same time that it was the most intense encounter with the real. In short, the notion of historical possibility dominated the discursive field of Du Bois's work, as well as the

entire interpretive enterprise of black cultural theorization. Because it was set aside, black culture could, by virtue of the very act of discrimination, become culture, insofar as, historically speaking, it was forced to turn its resources of spirit toward negation and critique.[17]

In this turning toward negation and critique (as analogous to the concealment of profound meaning from the oppressor that one finds in the practice of counterpoetics in Glissant's sense), for Spillers, black culture defines itself as critical practice at the expense of the production of a positive culture. This can be said to be the case for many colonized cultures. As I have been suggesting, rethinking the author as a figure of expression who draws on and extols the discourses and linguistic practices of her community is essential here, not (or not only) as a return to the traditional storyteller but insofar as this return might rearticulate what it is to say author as such. The author, then, would not be dead, but in so far as their willful intention aimed at a specific community, they would manifest the spirit of the griot. The author is not dead, so long as they bear with them the spirit of the storyteller.

Notes

1. Barthes, "The Death of the Author," 143.
2. Anshuman Mondal, *Racism and "Free Speech,"* London: Bloomsbury 2025, xvi.
3. Walter Benn Michaels, *The Shape of the Signifier: 1967 to the End of History*. Princeton: Princeton University Press, 2004; Kathleen Stock, *Only Imagine: Fiction, Interpretation, and Imagination*. Oxford University Press, 2017.
4. Cornel West to Edward Said, 16 November 1978. Edward Said Papers MS 1524. Box 5, Folder 9.
5. Cornel West to Edward Said, 16 November 1978. Edward Said Papers MS 1524. Box 5, Folder 9. Original emphasis.
6. Ernest J. Wilson III., "Orientalism: A Black Perspective," in *Journal of Palestine Studies*, 10, 2 (1981): 59–69, 69.
7. Michel Foucault, *The Order of Things: An Archeology of the Human Sciences*. New York: Vintage, 1973, 387.
8. Sylvia Wynter, "Beyond the Word of Man: Glissant and the New Discourse of the Antilles," in *World Literature Today*, 63, 4 (1989) 637–647, 643.

9. Wynter, "Beyond the Word of Man," 639.
10. Harris, "The Writer and Society," *Tradition, The Writer and Society*, 60.
11. Edward Kamau Brathwaite, *History of the Voice: The Development of Nation Language in Anglophone Caribbean Poetry*, London: New Beacon, 1984, 5–9.
12. Brathwaite, *History of the Voice*, 17.
13. Brathwaite, *History of the Voice*, 17.
14. Brathwaite, *History of the Voice*, 18–19.
15. Wynter, "Beyond the Word of Man," 640.
16. Hortense Spillers, "The Idea of Black Culture," *CR: The New Centennial Review*, 6, 3 (2006): 7–28, 25.
17. Spillers, "The Idea of Black Culture," 26.

Index

A
Antillo-Guyanese Front, 45
Arnold, Matthew, 6, 24
 disinteredness, 6

B
Balzac, Honoré de, 8, 9
Barthes, Roland, 2, 3, 5, 7–13, 17, 23, 24, 31, 40, 45, 50, 61, 63, 68, 78, 90, 93, 94, 99, 101, 102
 death of the author, 2, 4, 5, 7, 13, 95
 founder of language, 13
Batinist School, 81
Beardsley, Monroe C., 6, 7, 9, 13, 40, 80
Brathwaite, Kamau, 23, 99–101, 103

C
Conrad, Joseph, 84–87
Cordovan Zahirite school, 81
Creole/creolité, 50, 54

D
departmentalisation, 17, 44
Depestre, René, 36
Derrida, Jacques
 deconstruction, 50, 69, 71
 différance, 40, 51
 logocentricism, 43, 50, 71

F
Fanon, Frantz, 3, 5, 17, 19, 22, 27, 29, 30, 32, 33, 35, 36, 55, 58, 83, 88, 96, 98
Foucault, Michel, 10–13, 18, 22, 41, 48, 50, 68–71, 73, 76, 85, 86, 97, 100
 author function, 18, 45
Front de Libération Nationale (FLN, Algeria), 29

G
Gallop, Jane, 13
Gates Jr., Henry Louis, 20
Glissant, Édouard

alluvium, 42, 43, 75
counterpoetics, 55, 98, 102
forced poetics, 55–57, 100, 101
on decolonization, 19, 20
opacity, 22, 41–43, 55–58, 61, 64
open boat, 42, 46
poetic intention, 22, 40–42, 45, 48, 78, 95
poetics of relation, 22, 60
Tout-Monde, 20, 46, 57
Gopal, Priyamvada, 19, 25
decolonization, 19

H
Harris, Wilson, 3, 5, 7, 17, 22, 30–32, 94, 99
Hegel, G.W.F., 58–60, 73
humanism, 27–30, 32, 33, 48, 50, 69, 88, 89, 94
new humanism, 27, 29, 33

I
intention (in literature), 41
intentional fallacy, 6, 14

K
Kristeva, Julia, 20
intertextuality, 20

L
Leane, Jeanine, 10, 24
Lucashenko, Melissa, 10, 24
Lukacs, Gyorgy, 7, 14
historico-philosophical, 14

N
Négritude, 51–53, 60
New Critics, 6, 14

Q
Quimboiseur, 45, 94, 95, 101

R
Rushdie, Salman, 1–4
Ryan, Judith, 13, 14

S
Said, Edward, v, 3, 16, 19, 24, 67, 72, 91, 92, 102
beginning intention, 76–78, 95
filiation/affiliation, 3, 23, 74
Sartre, Jean-Paul, 69
Senghor, Léopold Sédar, 34, 51–53, 55, 57, 58, 60, 99
rhythm, 51, 56, 60, 61
Shaman, 8, 10, 45, 95
signifier/signified, 21, 51–53, 60, 61, 99
Smith, Zadie, 5, 12, 14, 24
Sollers, Philippe, 70
Spivak, Gayatri Chakravorty, 18, 27, 28, 30
Storyteller, 11, 34, 46, 87, 95, 99, 102

T
transatlantic slave trade, 47

V
Vico, Giambattista, 73, 74, 76

W
Walcott, Derek, 43, 48
Wimsatt, William K., 6, 7, 13, 80
Wynter, Sylvia, 23, 97, 98, 100, 101

GPSR Compliance

The European Union's (EU) General Product Safety Regulation (GPSR) is a set of rules that requires consumer products to be safe and our obligations to ensure this.

If you have any concerns about our products, you can contact us on ProductSafety@springernature.com

In case Publisher is established outside the EU, the EU authorized representative is:

Springer Nature Customer Service Center GmbH
Europaplatz 3
69115 Heidelberg, Germany

Batch number: 08246455

Printed by Printforce, the Netherlands